The white bell tower pierced the pure blue sky above the town of San Sebastian. A hot, dry wind swept from the valleys and across the hills bringing a bitter dust to the small Mexican town.

Alone on the steps of the chapel sat the boy, Jack Mason, sweat pouring from his brow, his face almost black with trail dust clinging to his skin.

Peurto Vallarta is less than a morning's ride, he thought to himself, picturing the blue waters of the Pacific and imagining the cool relief of dropping himself from the pier into their depths. Of course it wasn't to be; the gang had no purpose riding to Vallarta, no more than Jack did going inside to shelter from the rising midday heat. Jack's purpose was to sit on the steps of the chapel and wait.

At seventeen years, Jack was still a boy, but a man to be feared. At sixteen he'd relished the fame, the respect shown to him; Jack enjoyed the legends and myths that circulated the gang and spread out into the rest of Alta California. Down here in San Sebastian, Jack's name didn't bring fear, but it didn't need to. The group of white faced men who rode into town brought fear enough, they were clearly dangerous, the people of San Sebastian didn't have to know who they were – they'd find out soon enough.

Twelve chimes of the single bell that hung above the town signaled noon. Its ring echoed from the stone houses and mud coated shacks that made up this little town. *These folk must live real simple, real quiet,* Jack pondered to himself, almost envious of their existence. Less that twelve months previous and Jack would have laughed at the idea of settling in a place like this. But Jack had changed, he wanted something different now, and his reasoning was plain to see, Elena.

The heavy wooden doors of the chapel swung open and a thick, rough looking gunman pulled himself out into the sun.

"Looks like the padre's gone opened his mouth," he grumbled.

"Yeah?"

"Leon's pissed off, you can imagine."

"Yeah..." Jack knew where this was going.

"God damn this town is a shithole", the gunman offered. "You imagine livin' in a dump like this?" Jack barely opened his mouth to respond; this wasn't the kind of question that needed a response.

"No chance."

The thought of what was about to occur inside the chapel made Jack's heart sink. It wasn't sadness, nor regret, it was exhaustion; Jack had worn tired of this routine.

"Leon wants you to go inside", the gunman explained. "I'm to take watch out here."

Without a word, Jack lifted himself from the steps and made his way towards the chapel doors. The all too familiar sound of a cork being pulled from a bottle made it clear to Jack exactly what most of these men took 'taking watch' to mean.

"You need your wits about you. Put the bottle away", Jack's instruction was clear and stern but without even a hint of threat or need to raise his voice.

"It's just a little whiskey", the gunman retorted.

Jack stopped and turned to look at him. He didn't need to say anything more. The gunman corked the bottle and returned it to his sack – his eyes darting to the floor to avoid the embarrassment of catching Jack's glance. Though best part of twenty years older than Jack, this gunman knew his place.

Inside the chapel Theodore Leon lent quietly on the stone font. His thick beard and straggling hair covered most of his face. The little expression that could be seen from behind this mop was creased and concerned. Though rough, weathered and approaching fifty, Leon was

JETHRO COMPTON

THE FRONTIER TRILOGY

AND ADDITIONAL SHORT STORIES

SERVING THEATRE

S F

SINCE 1830

WWW.SAMUELFRENCH.CO.UK
WWW.SAMUELFRENCH.COM

ISBN 978-0-573-11104-4

www.samuelfrench.co.uk
www.samuelfrench.com

FOR AMATEUR PRODUCTION ENQUIRIES

UNITED KINGDOM AND WORLD EXCLUDING NORTH AMERICA

plays@SamuelFrench-London.co.uk

020 7255 4302/01

UNITED STATES AND CANADA

info@SamuelFrench.com

1-866-598-8449

Each title is subject to availability from Samuel French, depending upon country of performance.

For my parents; without whose generosity, support, and attic, *The Frontier* would never have been written.

Author's note

It was a sense of unfinished business that led me to sit down and write *The Frontier Trilogy*; a feeling that there was so much in the world of the American West that I was yet to explore – characters, landscapes and themes that I was yet to put on paper.

In 2013 I wrote my first Western for the stage, based on the short story by Dorothy M. Johnson, *The Man Who Shot Liberty Valance*. In that one play I tried to force every element of the genre I had grown to love onscreen, trying at once to achieve the glory of the High Noon and grit of Leone. Westerns are incredibly varied; in style, tone and content, there is not one the same. *Liberty* was never meant to be an homage to the genre, but in the very act of trying to adapt something so rarely seen on stage it was impossible to avoid replicating the themes, ideas and sometimes clichés of the Western.

As the pages ran by and the word count ran lower, I realised there were going to be so many aspects of life in nineteenth-century America that simply wouldn't find a home in the script. *Liberty* captured so many elements of the Wild West as we have come to know it, however fictionalised and exaggerated it might be, but many subjects of my fascination with the world are only briefly touched upon – the distant sound of a steam train is about as close as we came to the railroad.

Writing in a genre creates a number of constraints, whether that's due to an audience's perception of the world in which you're writing, or the fear of creating a pastiche, there were various things I was keen to avoid. But within these constraints the stories come together more easily, with greater clarity and often simplicity. A blank page is a terrifying prospect, but by framing that page in the world of the Western creates a much clearer route for the play to develop and for bold, adventurous choices to be made. Ironically, the very constraints become the key to the stories' freedom.

Each of the three volumes of *The Frontier* began life in scripture; the Bible contains universal stories that exist in almost every religious text and society across the world. I felt the marriage of these two worlds was the perfect setting for the fast paced, allegorical dramas I had envisaged. The plays now bear little resemblance to their

Biblical origins, but just as the genre narrowed options, so too did using these stories as a starting point.

In the additional stories, I looked to expand the world of the plays. The first, *San Sebastian*, was written in the days where *The Rattlesnake's Kiss* had got the better of me, and I chose to write the characters' origins rather than stare eternally at a blank page. In writing the character of young Jack Mason in *San Sebastian*, his motivations in *Rattlesnake* became so much clearer and fuelled the play's underlying message.

There are various themes across the trilogy that could easily run on and on, subplots that perhaps aren't entirely resolved, references to characters or worlds beyond those in the plays and stories. With each new story my intention was to bring a sense of closure for the audience, and yet, so long as one character survives, each tale feels as if it were only one episode in a far greater journey.

So long as I am happy to put some of these characters to rest, or to know that a bloodline may not have been ended, *The Frontier* will come to a close. And yet, in the nearly fifty thousand words across the five stories, there are still ideas, characters and themes from the American West that I've yet to touch upon. Perhaps it is this that leaves me with a sense of unfinished business. I never set out to be a writer of Western fiction, *Liberty* was the first, but if this feeling of unfinished business is anything to go by, I fear *The Frontier* may not be the last.

Jethro Compton
2015

Jethro Compton is a writer, director and independent theatre producer. His most notable productions include the acclaimed First World War triptych, *The Bunker Trilogy*, and the world premiere of *The Man Who Shot Liberty Valance*.

THE FRONTIER TRILOGY was first produced by Jethro Compton Productions at the Edinburgh Fringe Festival in August, 2015 with the following cast:

Blood Red Moon
LEVI HIL   Jonathan Mathews
ENOCH HILL   Sam Donnelly
ANNELISE FISCHER   Bebe Sanders
FATHER MANOAH   Chris Huntly-Turner

The Clock Strikes Noon
BENJAMIN 'BEN' WALKER   Sam Donnelly
SHERRIF FELIX JACKSON   Jonathan Mathews
LILLIAN 'MISS LILY' DAVENPORT   Bebe Sanders
FATHER MANOAH   Chris Huntly-Turner

The Rattlesnake's Kiss
FATHER MANOAH   Chris Huntly-Turner
US MARSHAL   Jonathan Mathews
ELENA   Bebe Sanders
SILAS   Sam Donnelly
JACK MASON   Chris Huntly-Turner
THEODORE LEON   Sam Donnelly

Directed by **Jethro Compton**
Costumes **Jessica Knight**
Sound **Ella Wahlström** in association with
Dylan Winn-Davies
Set and lighting **Jethro Compton**
Music **Jonny Sims**
Production Manager **Ben Karakashian**
Stage Manager **Maeve Bolger**

Contents

San Sebastian

A short story prequel to
The Rattlesnake's Kiss

a strong and handsome man. His eyes were piercing blue and pure white, unlike the jaundiced tint that occupied the gaze of most of his compandres.

He observed as young Jack entered the dark chapel and allowed his pupils to adjust to the gloom. Between Leon and Jack stood a dozen men, all equally rough and weathered, who formed an integral part of the Veneno Gang. The Venenos was the life's work of Theodore Leon. They were more feared and respected than any border gang from California to Texas. No one would refuse them, no one would threaten them, no lawman would challenge them. Of course, here in San Sebastian, so far south in Mexico, the rules were different.

Jack was loitering at the back of the chapel. *What's got into that boy?* Leon worried.

"Kid", Leon called out. "Kid, I want you to come down here. I want you to see what goes on here."

Silently but with visible reluctance, Jack made his way down the aisle to stand with the other men. On the floor before them, beneath the altar, on his knees, was the priest. An old man with wild white strings of hair that looked at odds with his dark skin.

"This here is the padre. He's been tellin' us 'bout how he's gone and informed the Governor that we've been residin' in his little town."

They knew this before they'd even arrived at the chapel. This was part of Leon's act, his love for the theatrical, he played ignorant and relished in the false hope it offered. Jack had seen it countless times.

The Venenos had been waiting in San Sebastian for three nights. They had been drinking and entertaining themselves with the local women. That afternoon a wagon would be coming through the town on its way east to Guajalarja. The wagon would contain supplies delivered to the docks at Puerto Vallarta. Among those supplies were to be enough cases of dynamite to separate Alta California from the continent – it was an opportunity too good to miss for Leon, who had recently invested in the lucrative and legitimate industry of ore mining.

The night before, just as the sun had gone down over Mexico, one of Leon's men had spotted a boy, no more than ten years old, running from the chapel in the direction of Vallarta. From a distance, he followed the boy through the night right the way into the port town and to the steps of the Governor's mansion.

When the Venenos woke that morning they were surprised to see their compadre galloping along the track into town – having assumed he was holed up with one of the senioritas. The news he brought was unwelcome but well rewarded.

And now Leon was casually leaning against the stone font in the chapel of Santo Sebastian with his men surrounding the priest who had betrayed them. The priest had no loyalty to the Venenos, to Leon, but Leon expected it nonetheless.

"Please, Signor Leon, I was only doing best for my town. I meant no harm to come to you or your men," the padre pleaded for mercy.

"I understand," Leon's voice, to be fair, was understanding. "I know you ain't meant for nothin' bad. You was just doin' right by your people."

A glimmer of relief shone in the padre's eyes. No such relief could be seen in Jack's, for he knew all too well the script from which Leon was reading. And Leon performed the lines well; sadness and remorse filled his voice as if it were one word from cracking with emotion. In another life, Jack always thought, Leon would have made himself a decent career in the playhouses of Sacramento.

"You must understand though, padre," here it was, "that I must also do what's best by my people."

The hope began to fade.

"As the leader of this gang it is my responsibility to ensure the safety of my men, to ensure their protection and that of their women and children."

"Of course but –"

"One of the best ways to ensure that safety is to make sure I have men who can fight. Take little Jack here, for instance. Step forward Jack."

Jack reluctantly pulled himself forward through the men so as to be standing in front of the priest. As with the rest of the charade, this part too was well rehearsed.

"This kid here, little Jack Mason, is the best shot you're like to find anywhere in this here land," continued Leon. "I bring him along with us coz if you get into a fight he's the best fella to have around. This kid is almost the best protection a man could ask for. You know what's better protection that this kid, padre?"

The priest shook his head, silent tears running down his cheeks. Jack lifted his eyes to the wooden carved crucifix that adored the crumbling white wall – he couldn't look at the man.

"What's better protection from men who might wanna fight is makin' sure they don't want to fight no more." Leon explained, "You see, you can have the best shot in Mexico ridin' alongside you into trouble, but hell, there's still a chance a piece of lead is gonna come whizzin' in your direction 'fore the kid here has a chance to take that man down. But if that man don't never fire that lead, he don't even raise his gun to you, well surely that's even better?"

The priest's silent tears hit the cold stone floor beneath him. Jack could see the man was broken, but Leon continued with the scene nonetheless.

"You know what stops a man from raisin' his gun, padre? Fear. Fear is the best protection a fella could ask for. So when I'm thinkin' about protectin' my men, my people, I know it's fear gonna keep 'em safe."

Jack had played his part; his performance was over. He shrank back into the crowd of armed men who, like salivating dogs waiting for a cut of meat, gazed on at the unfolding drama before them. Just like Jack, they'd seen it all before, countless times, but just like Jack as a child once he'd demanded the story of Theseus and Minotaur before bed, the men relished each and every word as if being heard for the first time.

Once hidden from the old man by the crowd of Venenos, Jack walked quietly around the chapel. Being raised in a gang of outlaws, he had little time for religion and the fear of God yet he'd always been fascinated by the buildings, particularly in Mexico where the white stone walls offered their own climate within.

Jack stopped at an old fresco on the wall. Time had worn it to appear as almost nothing more than a stain.

"What's that?" a small voice came from behind him.

"A painting," Jack whispered his response. This was too much attention to be drawing away from the priest's trouble.

"It don't look very good," the voice came again. Jack turned to the little boy who stood beside him. Peter, his brother, not yet ten years old.

"It's old," he informed him. "You shouldn't be in here. You should wait back at the cantina."

Theodore Leon felt no age was too young to begin your induction into the Venenos. Peter was testament to that. At nine years of age he had already witnessed enough violence and horror to last him a lifetime.

"Leon said I was allowed to see it."

"You ain't gonna like it." A year ago, the first time Peter road out with the gang on the back of Jack's horse, Jack had relished the chance to share this world with his little brother. At home Jack was nothing special, but out on the road he became the man he was in the stories, the gunslinger. A year ago he wanted to show off to his little brother but now he wanted Peter to be as far from that life as possible – now he just wanted Elena.

"Fella outside said Leon's gonna use the venom on him," Peter chimed, cheerfully.

"He ain't wrong there," Jack's response captured his exhaustion.

"Don't you want to see that?"

"No I don't," he responded sternly, "and neither do you."

"Leon says I can."

"Just coz he says you can don't mean you have to." Jack had spent his whole life looking up to Leon and his men and wanting to be just like them. Perhaps if he'd had himself for an older brother he would have known better than to follow Leon blindly. Jack saw it now as his responsibility to ensure Peter knew there was a choice, to give him the chance to get away from it all.

" What's the paintin' meant to be anyways? " Peter asked.

" It's Saint Sebastian, the fella the town's named after. "

" How come they named a town after him? "

" Coz he's a saint."

"How come he's a saint?"

"Coz he's a martyr."

"A what?" Peter clearly wanted an answer and an end to the conversation on the old painting.

" He got himself killed for believin' in God. "

" Stupid thing to get killed over. "

" Yeah. "

The night before when Leon's men had been drinking whiskey and taking advantage of the local hospitality, Jack had been sat quietly out in the square when a young girl had brought out a drink. He made an effort of speaking to her nicely, he didn't know her, he didn't necessarily want to know her, but he wanted her to know that he wasn't like the rest of the Venenos.

" What's the name of your town mean? " he'd asked politely.

"Santo Sebastian,"came the girl's reply as she explained the story of Sebastian who had been murdered in Roman times for his Christian beliefs. " They say he was chained to a tree and his flesh was filled with arrows. "

" I'd like to die for somethin' I believe", Jack thought aloud. The Mexican girl smiled strangely as if she'd not quite understood his meaning.

"You believe in God? " she asked.

" No. "

" Then what? "

" I... " he thought, " I ain't sure yet. "

" You must find it soon", her advice was confident despite the potential danger she was in, " or you will die without knowing it. "

"Why might I die?"

"You are outlaws, yes? You could die tomorrow."

"That right?" he smiled.

"If you don't have God then you could die tomorrow for nothing."

"I have somethin'."

"What?" she seemed genuinely intrigued.

"It ain't God." The smile broadened on his face.

"I see", she joined his smile. "She must be very beautiful."

"Yeah, she is."

"Then why are you here? Why do you risk everything you have for money? If you are shot here tomorrow you could die in Santo Sebastian and never see her again." Her argument was compelling.

"I don't have an answer," Jack conceded.

"Then perhaps you need to ask yourself the question until you do." With that, the girl left Jack alone in the square; the moonlight reflecting brightly from the walls of the church and the surrounding houses.

All the doubts and concerns Jack had been feeling in the previous months seemed to come together in his mind. The short conversation with that girl played in his mind over and over through the night and, just as she said, he asked himself the question, again and again. By morning, he wondered if that Mexican girl had even existed, or had been conjured from a foul mixture of whiskey and tequila.

As Leon withdrew the blade from the priest's tongue, he looked for Jack and Peter in the crowd of men only to see them across the church staring at a stain on the wall. He'd wanted Peter to see this; a flash of rage tore across his face before he settled it. Whatever fear or doubt had worked itself into Jack's mind was causing trouble, and it would cause more trouble still, Leon knew this.

"Any of you fellas want to make your peace with the Lord," Leon announced to the gang of cackling dogs, "now's your chance. The wagon is gonna pull through town in less than two hours and I'm guessin' it's gonna be accompanied by a few extra of the Governor's men. So let's be ready for them."

Leon marched through the crowd towards the doors.

"Jack, you're with me," he ordered without even a glance. "Peter, you're to stay out the way."

"I can take care of myself," Peter's response was brave and defiant.

"You'll stay out the way, goddammit." Leon's rage scared Peter more than the idea of a gunfight, but Jack knew it was aimed at him. Jack knew they should have watched Leon cut the Priest's tongue because that's what Leon would have wanted, but it wasn't what Jack wanted and that's exactly what he'd come to learn – they weren't the same thing.

"You go back to the cantina, Peter," Jack instructed. "I'll be gone with Leon for a few hours. You just wait for us."

"I want to fight 'longside the men."

"No you don't."

"I do!"

"If you knew what it was to fight alongside the gang and take a man's life, you wouldn't want to," there was sadness to Jack's voice. "Please, Peter, go back to the cantina."

"I'll get my chance," Peter stormed away. "One day I'll get my chance rather'n sit and hide with the women. I'll fight the lawmen just like you and Leon."

"I hope not." Jack followed his little brother out into the bright sunlight. His eyes burned as the pure white subsided. Leon was already mounted on his horse, a small looking glass was held over one eye, gazing in the direction of Puerto Vallarta.

Jack moved to the stables where a Mexican boy collected his horse. The boy couldn't have been much younger than Jack, but he looked to the ground in fear as he handed him the reins.

"Gracias", Jack offered. The attempt to calm the boy's nerves didn't work and he lowered his head even further towards the ground.

A pang of guilt spread through Jack's gut. He thought for a moment of the suffering the Venenos had brought on this little town, he thought of what had happened to the stable boy's sisters and mother. Jack took no pride in the suffering of others, especially innocents. He'd always seen it as the price for the life the Venenos led, that for men to live in such a way must cause suffering to others. But as his desire for that life faded, the outcome of its consequences became almost unbearable to him.

"I'm sorry..." this was even less successful; the boy began to tremble.

Jack climbed onto the horse and pushed it forwards and back out into the light. He kept his eyes forward, his face flush with embarrassment as he chastised himself for even opening his mouth.

Jack and Leon sat atop a hill half a mile west of San Sebastian overlooking the road that led to the ocean. Through the looking glass Jack could almost make out the moment where the blue of the water mixed with the sky.

What I'd give to swim in that water with the sun on my back, he could almost feel its cool relief just from the thought of it.

"Do I have your attention, kid?" Leon interrupted his daydreaming.

"Course."

"I need you alert, Jack," Leon continued. "I ain't lookin' to get myself shot in this shitty little town in Mexico. You understand?"

"You got my attention. I'm alert." It was true, no matter how Jack felt about the life he'd chosen, he wasn't about to let it end here in the Mexican dust, a week's ride from Elena.

Leon took the glass from Jack and trained it along the road.

"They're comin'", he announced.

Jack removed his hat, held it high above and signaled back towards San Sebastian. In the church bell tower one of the Venenos signaled to the rest of the men. Once by one, they emerged from their resting spots and took position atop the church and buildings of the small town. There was no doubt, when the wagon approached from Puerto Vallarta accompanied by the Governor's men, they'd see the Venenos waiting for them. All the Venenos, as plain as the night sky, stood out in the afternoon sun. All the Venenos, except Jack and Leon, who would wait until the wagon rolled past and make their move.

"We best move away from the ridge", Jack decided.

"We got some minutes yet 'fore they're on us", Leon seemed unconcerned by the approaching posse.

Jack hadn't been left alone with him since they crossed the border. He found it uncomfortable as he tried to find words to fill the silence. Luckily for him it was Leon who found them.

"I hear you been spending time with young Elena."

"Some," Jack tried to keep his voice steady.

"She's a fine girl," Leon offered.

"She is." Jack's heart was thumping in his chest so hard he feared Leon would hear it.

"Want my advice, kid?"

"Course."

"Don't spend too much time with the same woman – find variety."

"I ain't growin' tired of her," Jack defended before reminding himself to keep calm.

"Ain't worried you're growin' tired, kid. Easy for a man to grow confused, is what I'm sayin'."

"I don't follow."

"She's a whore, Jack", Leon stated calmly. "She's paid to make men happy, to keep 'em happy. You go to bed with her every night and eventually the night you see her with another man your gut is gonna turn to rot. It ain't healthy to fall in love with a whore, it's easy, but it ain't healthy."

Jack couldn't find any words. The gut rot Leon had described was already consuming Jack from this very conversation.

"She's a sweet enough girl, Jack, but there's plenty sweet girls in the camp. You best find another one 'fore you grow too attached to her."

All in the same moment Jack was filled with humiliation, anger and pride. Yes Elena was a working girl, she had serviced almost every man in the Venenos from one time to another, but this was different. Whatever Leon might think of Elena, Jack knew the truth – it was love. Less than a month previous, Jack had lain in her arms and told Elena of his feelings. Her response, Jack was sure of it, was no charade; she had fallen for him as he had for her.

"Let's get out of sight", Leon's words returned Jack's mind to the task at hand. "You ready for them?"

"I'm ready."

The two men pushed their horses back from the edge of the ravine, out of sight from the road below. Jack climbed of his mare and tied the reins to an old fence.

"You clear on the plan?" Leon questioned.

"I'm clear."

"Tell it to me."

"I'm told you I'm clear," Jack's impatience was the closest Leon had ever seen him to insolence. He wasn't impressed.

"It's a dangerous thing to believe the stories men tell about you. You know that, kid? Folk talk about the young Jack Mason with a shot faster than any alive, folk talk on how he's invincible. But you ain't, kid. You ain't invincible. And you ain't the leader of this gang yet – I am. So when I tell you to do somethin' you damn well do it, or I'll smack you across the face 'til you do. Understand?"

Jack nodded without looking Leon in the eye.

"So tell me," Leon continued. "Tell me the plan."

"Let the wagon pass. Climb down and follow it. Locate which trailer's containin' goods and which is containin' Governor's men. 'Fore it gets to town I'm to dispatch the men. Our boys will finish what's left of them when they make it into San Sebastian."

"Good." Leon knew Jack would be clear on the plan, but the distance that had grown between the two of them concerned him. Whatever it was that had clouded Jack's mind, Leon wasn't going to risk it getting in the way of business.

Jack checked his revolvers, one on each hip, and pulled a repeater from the horse's saddle. Six shots in each revolver, eight in the repeater. Twenty shots before he'd need to reload. With Jack's record for accuracy, twenty shots meant twenty men.

Crouching down so as almost on all fours, he made his way back towards the ridge. The trap was set. As Jack waited for the ambush, he thought again of the girl he had met outside the cantina. He could die here in this Mexican dirt and never see Elena again. And for what? He still didn't have an answer.

In the back of a carriage, far below the ridge along the road, a group of soldiers huddled beneath the canvas frame, nervously waiting. The Governor had come to them that morning and warned of the proposed ambush at Santo Sebastian. Their heavy uniforms fair outweighed the benefits of travelling in the shade, and sweat poured from their skin.

At the front of the wagon sat their sergeant, roasting in the afternoon sun despite the fact his uniform had been left back in Puerto Vallarta and his wore instead the clothes of a civilian. A disguise he thought would be enough to pass him off as a tradesman and gain him valuable moments when they turned the tables on this group of border thieves.

There was nothing unusual to the sergeant about this task; all too often had he been requested to accompany high value goods across this lawless land. What made this occasion unique, however, was the volatility of their cargo. He'd begged the Governor to simply wait until the route was clear before shipping the dynamite, but the Governor refused to delay his business at the whim of bandits. So here they were, one carriage full of grain, one of cloth, one of explosives and one of soldiers.

The sergeant knew they had the upper hand – the element of surprise was in their favor. When the American thieves showed themselves, the wagon would stop and the sergeant and other drivers would surrender immediately, when the canvas was pulled back on the first cart, the bandits would discover their bounty, on the second, they'd meet their death.

The white walls of Santo Sebastian slowly rose out of the dirt as the wagon moved steadily up the road. Atop the buildings the sergeant could see the figures of armed men, waiting. This couldn't be better; he'd feared the Americans might wait until the wagon was in town before showing themselves – in a moment of panic it's far more likely guns start to go off and people get themselves killed before the plan can be rolled out.

The army issue revolver under his jacket felt hot and heavy as the moment of its need grew nearer. A sliver of doubt crossed his mind at his decision not to have an armed escort in sight of the thieves; *Surely they will anticipate some resistance?* But an armed guard would only have led to more fingers on triggers, more chance of their ambush going awry.

He counted the men who lined the rooftops and outer walls of the town. At least eleven – no match for the dozen trained soldiers hidden in the second carriage, even if there are some more waiting for us.

As the town grew nearer, sweat worked its way down his palms and onto his fingers. His eyes stung from the blinding sunlight reflecting from the white, almost mirage-like, town. *Stay calm, stay in control.*

A single gunshot rang out and echoed around the hills that surrounded them. The sergeant's heart raced; he looked to the town for signs that someone had fired a warning shot. No smoke that he could see, no weapons raised.

A second shot rang out. There was no doubting from where it came; the sergeant swung his head round and lifted himself up to see over his cart. The sight filled him with fear.

The second wagon had stopped twenty feet behind; the horse that had pulled it lay crumpled in the dust. On its other side, far along the road to Puerto Vallarta stood the two wagons containing grain and cloth, stopped in their tracks. The sergeant could just make out the drivers of both wagons, both Governor's men, slumped over and stained in the blood from their own throats. *They knew we were coming... This is the ambush,* the realization almost took his legs from under him. Fumbling, panicking, he reached his sweat soaked fingers inside his jacket to draw his revolver.

In the time since the first shot had broken the afternoon's peace, hell had unleashed itself from the back of the second carriage. Soldiers jumped from beneath the canvas, weapons drawn, but were dead before they hit the ground. Single, calm, steady shots pierced the air and dropped the soldiers into the dirt.

The sergeant took aim back down the road, his revolver level but shaking with the fear that coursed down his arm. There was nothing to aim at. Just as the sergeant could not find a target, nor could the men whose rifles were aimed in all directions from gaps in the canvas.

As the cacophony of screams and gunshots faded into the quiet groans of dying men, the sergeant saw him. The boy stepped out from behind the wagon just twenty feet from him. One boy had just slaughtered a dozen trained soldiers.

The sergeant placed his sights on the boy. At twenty feet, the shot was easy. He steadied his breath, he calmed his nerves, he took the shot.

Theodore Leon sat on his horse above the ravine and looked down on the scene of utter chaos and destruction as the Mexican took his shot. The revolver flashed violently in the soldier's hand as it backfired, sending shards of bullet and steel in all directions in a cloud of gunpowder and flame.

Before the sound had even reached Leon's ears the entire ravine seemed engulfed in a vicious inferno as the wagon of dynamite, catching the sparks from the shattered peacemaker, detonated instantly.

"Son of a bitch!" his voice echoed and blended with the sound of the explosion that rang out below. He pushed his horse forward sharply and led it down a steep track to the road.

The Venenos were hurriedly making their way down the road from the town. Their shouts and cries filled the air.

"Jack!" Leon called out through the dust and smoke that engulfed the road. "You out there, kid?"

Leon could barely see as he stepped over chunks of charred horseflesh and burning timber. As he neared the second wagon Leon saw Jack sat in the dirt leaning against the wheel.

"You hurt?" he called out.

"I'm fine." Jack's voice almost filled with laughter.

"What in the name of Jesus Christ happened?" Leon was raging.

"I'm guessin' the fella's gun misfired".

In the center of the road a black, smoking crater signposted the previous location of the wagon containing the dynamite. The wagon, its driver and horse now lay scattered in pieces across the road and in the surrounding brush. Leon's ears were ringing from the sound of the almighty blast; Jack's face was stained black with soot and dust.

"Jesus Christ…" Leon was almost lost for words.

"I reckon that's rotten luck", Jack couldn't hide his amusement, 'blowin' the whole wagon sky high on account of a faulty revolver."

"You find this funny?" Leon's rage was now directed fully at Jack. "This whole damn trip has been for nothin'. Our wages was in that wagon. That dynamite was worth a goddamn fortune and now it's gone up in smoke."

"All this killin' and we ain't got nothin' to show for it." There was a sadness beneath his laughter that was imperceptible to a man like Leon.

The rest of the men had arrived in the midst of the carnage.

" What's in them other two? " Leon pointed to the remaining wagons, discarded along the road.

" Supplies. Grain maybe. Nothing much of value. "

" Jesus fucking Christ! "

One of the men helped Jack to his feet and brushed him down.

"Amazed you ain't hurt, Jack, " the man offered through his thick, dust caked beard. " That was somethin' to behold, I tell you. Thought the fella had the drop on you and then up he goes into tiny pieces. "

" That was fine shootin', Jack, " offered another of the men.

" Too right, best I seen, " chimed in another.

" What was there, dozen of them?"

" All shot through ", then men continued, almost to themselves, beginning the tale that years later would grow to become legend. Across the years, some facts would fade, others would be embellished, and men would talk of the time Jack Mason took down an entire Mexican posse with only a revolver and six bullets. Jack took no pleasure in the men's praise.

As the smoke cleared Leon sent a handful of the gang to retrieve the wagons. *Grain and supplies is better than goin' back empty handed.*

Leon was a proud man and the idea of stories spreading of how the Venenos lost their bounty as a result of incompetence angered him greatly. He knew all too well the importance or reputation; it's what kept them in business.

" Unhook that beast from the wagon, " he ordered, pointing to the horse that lay dead attached to the soldiers' carriage. " Fix another one to it, bring it into town. I'm gonna leave these sons of bitch spiks somethin' to remember us by. "

Less than an hour later the Venenos departed Santo Sebastian, headed for the border. As they passed over a hill north of the town, Jack looked to the west, gazed at the glimmer of sea and imagined the day he could have had. *If I were a free man,* he thought.

When the Venenos road out they left behind them destruction and despair. Fathers and brothers cried for their women and daughters; the town wept for their padre's suffering; the road to Peurto Vallarta was stained with blood and ash; and in the center of the town, in their white walled square outside the church of Saint Sebastian, a pile of bloodied, skinless soldiers lay rotting in the heat.

" The shedding of skin allows for rebirth," Leon announced to the petrified crowd as they watched over the horrific butchering and desecration of the soldiers' bodies. " The snake sheds its skin to grow – to evolve. Just as the snake, these men are reborn. Until today they were representatives of your pathetic country, of the weakness of man. From this day forward they shall be become something far greater. These men now represent us, for when you hear our name, or your children hear our name, or your grandchildren hear the name Venenos, they will remember these bodies and they will remember the day your people stood in our way. I did not wish for any of this, believe me, but you have left me with little choice. I am fair and I am lenient, but when you cross the Venenos you will suffer the consequences."

Jack had stood in the shade of the chapel away from the gore of the main square. He listened to Leon's words with sadness but defiance – of everything he'd known in his life he'd never been as sure as he was of what he wanted now. He made a promise to himself in that moment to return to Elena, to ask for her hand, and to leave the Venenos and this life far behind. He vowed the next time he saw the sea he wouldn't simply dream of diving into its cool water.

From his vantage he observed his little brother, Peter, gazing on from a perch atop a small wall. The look in Peter's eyes was well known to Jack, he'd had it in his own eyes most of his life. Bloodlust. Revenge.

Jack thought of how he would save Peter from this life. But would he ever understand? He was too infatuated with the stories of death and glory; he was part of this world now.

As the gang road north, Leon pulled his horse alongside Jack's.

"You alright, kid?" he asked.

"Yeah."

"Yeah?" Leon was unconvinced. "The boys are right, that was some fine shootin' back there."

"Thanks."

"I been worried about you, kid. You been real quiet of late."

"Yeah." Jack looked to the man he'd spent his whole life admiring; there was nothing more to say.

"You sure everythin's alright?"

Jack thought over his answer with great care.

"It will be."

The End

The Frontier Trilogy: Volume I

Blood Red Moon

CHARACTERS

ENOCH HILL – The elder of the two brothers. 25-35. He is strong, proud, and stubborn, but he can be cruel.

LEVI HILL – The younger of the two. 20-30. He is kind-hearted, polite, and less confident than his brother.

ANNELISE FISCHER – A local girl. 20-30. She is gentle, honest, and kind.

FATHER MANOAH – The priest at The Chapel of Emmanuel. 20-25. Though young, he is calm, noble, and respected.

SETTING

The Chapel of Emmanuel, North of Canyon Falls, America
Winter 1855
&
The Valley of Ellah, West of St Emmanuel
Summer 1855

Prologue – The Chapel of Emmanuel

In the secluded chapel, night has descended. A soft red glow of moonlight pours in through the crucifix shaped window that stands above the altar. It illuminates the almost derelict building.

At the far end the doors swing open. A young man, **LEVI HILL**, *steps forward cautiously into the semi-darkness.* **LEVI** *is a young, healthy looking man, well dressed in his winter layers. He is alone. The chapel seems deserted.*

Crossing the chapel. He falls to his knees before the alter and begins to pray silently.

A noise startles him.

MANOAH There's no gold here.

LEVI Who's there?

MANOAH If you've come to steal from us, you'll find nothin' of value.

LEVI I ain't lookin' to steal. Just come to pray, is all.

MANOAH In the middle of the night?

LEVI I weren't of the understandin' the Almighty kept strict to business hours.

MANOAH But what about you? What prayer so desperate brings you to his house past sundown? What do you fear so great can't wait for morning?

LEVI There weren't no lights on. I took the place to be deserted. Why you stalkin' round in the dark for?

MANOAH For many years I have stumbled in the dark.

LEVI That some sort of allegory, father?

MANOAH No son.

> *He steps forward into the moonlight. A strip of black material covers his eyes. He is blind.*

> Means I haven't seen light in many years. Means I don't keep candles burning through the night.

LEVI I beg pardon, father. But you ain't got no fire burning or nothin'. It's bitter cold tonight.

MANOAH Winters here can be cruel.

LEVI I didn't mean to disturb.

MANOAH It's no disturbance. What's your name, son?

LEVI Levi Hill.

MANOAH You're not familiar to me, Levi.

LEVI I ain't been long in California. And your chapel is too far a ride.

MANOAH But you've made it tonight?

LEVI Yes, sir.

MANOAH Where have you travelled from?

LEVI Ellah Valley.

MANOAH That's a treacherous road by dark.

LEVI The night is illuminated, father. The moon's glowin' fierce red – ain't no darker than dawn. It's a fine sight.

MANOAH Luna de Sangre.

LEVI What's that?

MANOAH The blood moon.

LEVI Yeah?

MANOAH The people who occupied these lands before the white men came believed it to be an omen. The Mexicans call it Luna de Sangre. It's said the moon bleeds red in the sky as warning.

LEVI Warnin' of what, father?

MANOAH Murder.

Silence.

What brings you here, Levi?

Silence.

LEVI I don't know your name, father.

MANOAH Manoah.

LEVI How did you lose your sight, father?

MANOAH Many years ago.

LEVI But how?

Pause.

MANOAH It was taken from me.

LEVI By God?

> **MANOAH** *laughs.*

It's a crime you can't take in the beauty of tonight, father. Sure I ain't never seen a night like it. Wonder if there'll ever be another one again.

MANOAH You talk with a sadness, Levi.

LEVI Yeah?

MANOAH Is there something you fear?

Silence.

Levi?

LEVI No. No – I been afraid my whole life, father. But not tonight.

MANOAH What's changed?

LEVI I been afraid coz I ain't been able to make decisions. I been scared o' chosin' wrong. But not tonight – tonight I know exactly what I got to do.

MANOAH And what's that?

LEVI I gotta ask God's forgiveness.

MANOAH His forgiveness for what?

LEVI For the murder I am to commit.

Scene One – The Claim

*As the warm summer evening comes to an end, the two brothers, **ENOCH** and **LEVI**, arrive by the side of a small creek. **ENOCH** is stronger, more handsome and yet more worn than his younger brother.*

LEVI examines a map.

LEVI Accordin' to this it's everythin' west of the tree line, right to the other side of the valley.

ENOCH Will you put that thing away.

LEVI We gotta be certain.

ENOCH I am certain.

LEVI We pan in the wrong place and we'll find ourselves a whole lot of trouble.

ENOCH Put down the map and take a look around. Does this not look exactly as you'd imagined?

LEVI I guess. Yeah. This is just what I pictured.

ENOCH No wonder the Mexicans fought so hard not to let this land go. You ever seen anythin' so beautiful?

LEVI Not to my recollection.

ENOCH Nor mine.

LEVI Except perhaps Rosie.

ENOCH Rosie?

LEVI The servin' girl at the big house.

ENOCH Jesus, Levi. The homely lookin' thing?

LEVI She weren't so homely.

ENOCH She been any homelier and I'd have built her a sty and reared her for meat.

LEVI That ain't funny, Enoch.

ENOCH It ain't never meant to be funny neither. Just givin' you some truthful perspective, brother.

LEVI Ain't no need to be so cruel.

ENOCH You been thinkin' about her all the way from Richmond?

LEVI Not all the way.

ENOCH I promise you, brother, when we strike our fortune there'll be women by the dozen more beautiful and more eager than your carthorse Rosie.

LEVI She weren't so homely, were she?

ENOCH Really, brother?

LEVI I reckon she had nice eyes.

ENOCH Yeah, I'll give you that – she did have pretty eyes. Next time you see her you cut two holes in your horse blanket and toss it over her. She'll rival any woman alive.

> **LEVI** *laughs.*

What do you say we camp here for the night?

LEVI I reckon it's a fine spot. You want I should fix us somethin' to eat?

ENOCH Food can wait. It's time to celebrate. Fetch us a bottle of that corn liquor.

> **LEVI** *collects a bottle and two mugs from his pack. He pours for them both and they hold up their mugs for a toast.*

LEVI The end of our journey.

ENOCH No, brother – the beginning.

LEVI May the waters bring us good fortune.

They drink.

I wish mother could see this view.

ENOCH She will. Once we hit our strike we'll call for the both of them.

LEVI What about pa?

ENOCH Let him rest through the winter. In spring, when he's well enough to travel, we'll send for them.

LEVI Reckon the warmer climate will do him good.

ENOCH We'll build them their own home right up here so mother can see this view every mornin'. Get 'em some help so they don't have to worry none.

LEVI That'd be fine. I'd like that.

ENOCH Things are changin' for us, brother. I can feel it. We've done our time, had our share of sufferin', but no more. I'm tellin' you, this is the start for us.

LEVI I hope so Enoch. I truly do.

ENOCH That water looks damn cold. It's snow melt from up in the mountains. Melts and runs right down into the valleys.

LEVI Bet it tastes real fresh.

ENOCH Sure, so long as no one's been pissin' up there in the snow.

LEVI That's gonna be in my mind every time I go down there for a drink. Why d'you gotta spoil everythin' for me?

ENOCH That's what big brother's are for.

He laughs warmly.

What day is it?

LEVI Saturday, why?

ENOCH Let's take tomorrow to rest. I'm blistered from the saddle and could do with a day's peace. We'll start on Monday.

LEVI D'you see that chapel back before the hills?

ENOCH No.

LEVI It was out on its own – real remote.

ENOCH I saw the chapel just fine. I mean, no you ain't riddin' all the way out there.

LEVI Why not?

ENOCH You made it since Richmond without goin' to service. Why you need to start up with that again?

LEVI I'd just feel better, is all.

ENOCH You got your book, ain't you?

LEVI It ain't the same. And 'sides, I might meet some locals up there.

ENOCH Ha! Some lady folk perhaps? I should have guessed, brother, only you would disguise gettin' some strange as a holy quest for enlightenment.

LEVI That ain't what I meant.

ENOCH Perhaps you are my brother after all.

LEVI You never know who we might meet.

ENOCH Exactly. Don't want to go advertisin' our presence. People hear there's gold and they'll come take if from us.

LEVI But we have a title – it's our claim.

ENOCH You think that scrap of paper means anythin' to people out here? Then you're mistaken. They'd cut our throats and take the gold as easy as tip their hats and smile at a pretty girl.

LEVI It'll get awful lonely up here is we don't have no company.

ENOCH You tired of me already, little brother?

LEVI I don't mean that.

ENOCH Sure you can get on my nerves near enough for me to strangle you to death – but it ain't never lonely with the two of us.

LEVI Just in the long term –

ENOCH In the long term we'll find enough gold to get the claim protected, get the two of us safe. Then we'll think about entertainin' the neighbours. 'sides, I thought you hated the city, all them crowds?

LEVI I ain't after the city, but I don't want to 'come a hermit livin' out in the middle o' nowhere neither.

ENOCH Give it some time – then we'll find you some play friends.

LEVI I ain't after play friends.

ENOCH Then I'll get you whatever you want. Have I ever left you wantin' for somethin'?

LEVI No.

ENOCH That's right. You ever wanted a better big brother?

LEVI Course not.

ENOCH Then you give us some time. Afore long there won't be nothin' the two of us can't get if we want it.

LEVI I don't want no fancy life.

ENOCH You don't have to – just anythin' you want. Anythin' *we* want.

A comfortable silence.

LEVI Sun's gonna fall behind them hills soon.

ENOCH It'll be dark 'fore long. We should set up camp.

LEVI I reckon I'll sleep outside tonight. I'd like to see the stars.

ENOCH It'll be a good night for it.

LEVI I dreamed what the stars would look like in California. I imagined them more bright, but more spread out – more free.

ENOCH Reckon they'll look much the same.

LEVI You know what I mean. Everythin' out here seems better – more brilliant.

ENOCH Yeah.

Silence.

Any of that cornbread left?

LEVI You don't want somethin' hot?

ENOCH Just somethin' to soak up a little o' this rot. I wanna be in my cups but I ain't lookin' to piss myself in the night.

LEVI *laughs as he fetches cornbread from his pack. He hands it over.*

LEVI There you go.

ENOCH *takes a bite and grins.*

ENOCH Don't never tell mother, but I reckon your biscuits are easy gettin' better'n hers.

LEVI She'd smack you with pa's belt for that.

ENOCH That's why you ain't never gonna tell her.

LEVI You reckon she misses us?

ENOCH I dunno. You maybe.

LEVI She ain't never liked me better.

ENOCH Ha! No point tryin' to protect my feelin's, Levi.

LEVI Then why d'you want to bring her out here?

ENOCH I want prove to her the man I become. She always worried I was gonna turn out bad. I want her to see me here, with you, rich, a decent home, perhaps a wife. Then she'll look at me like she's looked at you all these years.

LEVI I never heard her say a bad word about you.

ENOCH She don't have to – it's in her eyes. Like I can't never do nothin' right. I'll show her though; I'll make her proud.

LEVI I can't wait to get started Monday.

ENOCH Don't be too anxious. Soon enough we'll both be sick tired of pannin' in that ice cold water.

LEVI Not so long as we remember that the work is for us. Ain't no boss here – ain't no one to answer to but you and me.

ENOCH That's right.

LEVI I'm gonna turn in.

ENOCH I'll finish the bottle.

LEVI I'm happy to be here with you, Enoch.

ENOCH Ain't no place better in the world. Good night, little brother.

LEVI Good night.

Scene Two – Gold

LEVI *is panning water for gold in the river. Many weeks have passed. He appears tired and frustrated as he sings to himself.*

LEVI

SHE TOLD ME SHE LOVED ME
THAT SHE'D STAY BY MY SIDE,
AND IN SPRINGTIME I PROMISED
I'D MAKE HER MY BRIDE

ENOCH *approaches. He listens from a distance.* **LEVI** *notices him.*

BUT THE WINTER WAS CRUEL,
AND HER CRUELER STILL,
BY SPRING SHE HAD LEFT ME
ALONE AND NOW ILL.

ENOCH I ain't heard you sing in weeks.

LEVI Guess there ain't been much to sing about.

ENOCH Why today then? You found somethin'?

LEVI Nothin'.

ENOCH It's out there. We just gotta find it.

LEVI Ain't seen so much as a cricket's dick o' gold in weeks.

ENOCH It's out there.

LEVI How can you be so sure?

ENOCH You ever known me to be wrong?

LEVI On occasion.

ENOCH Never.

LEVI This ain't trackin' boars, Enoch, this is different.

ENOCH Don't doubt, little brother. Doubt's the only thing can come 'tween a man and what he wants.

LEVI Sure – I ain't doubtin'. 'Sides, we're in good shape out here, plenty food and drink for us to get by.

ENOCH Get by?

LEVI Hunt in the woods for meat, endless supply of fresh water.

ENOCH I been gettin' by my whole life. I ain't come right 'cross the continent to get by. I come here for gold – for my fortune.

LEVI I know. Same as me.

ENOCH 'Cept you'd be happy just gettin' by.

LEVI I just meant 'til we find the gold.

ENOCH Gold?

LEVI Didn't you know? There's plenty o' gold in this here creek.

ENOCH That's more like it.

LEVI You wanna get down here and help me find it?

ENOCH You worried I ain't pullin' my weight, little brother?

LEVI Two of us workin' got twice the chance o' findin' it.

ENOCH Ain't you the mathematician.

LEVI I didn't mean nothin' by it.

ENOCH I been scrabblin' down in that creek same as you.

LEVI I know, brother.

ENOCH I been slavin' just as hard.

LEVI Please, Enoch, ain't no cause for you to lose your temper.

ENOCH It's my money funded this whole damn thing.

LEVI I know that.

ENOCH But you want me workin' on my hands and knees as well.

LEVI I didn't –

ENOCH Well here you go, little brother.

> **ENOCH** *grabs a handful of soil and throws it into* **LEVI***'s pan with a thud.*

There you are. There's my contribution. You know, there ain't no boss out here. I'll work when I damn well please.

LEVI Of course.

> **ENOCH** *storms away, muttering angrily under his breath.*

> **LEVI** *lowers his head, embarrassed. He sifts absentmindedly through the pan. He sees it, a small clump of shining metal.*

LEVI Enoch...

> **LEVI** *rubs soil from the little golden rock.*

ENOCH!

> **ENOCH** *returns angrily.*

ENOCH I ain't gonna apologise if I hurt your feelin's.

LEVI No. Look…

ENOCH If you can't stomach bein' spoken to like a man then –

LEVI ENOCH! Quit talkin' and take a look.

ENOCH Who the hell d'you think –

He sees the gold. He examines it closely.

Jesus Christ…

LEVI That's right.

ENOCH It's gold?

LEVI Sure is.

ENOCH What d'you reckon it weighs? Couple o' ounces?

LEVI At least.

ENOCH Where did it come from? Where d'you find it?

LEVI I didn't – you pulled it out of the water with your bare hands.

ENOCH It's a regular miracle. Jesus, Mary and Joseph. Where did I pull it out from?

LEVI Somewhere here.

ENOCH Pass me a pan.

They set to work. Very quickly **ENOCH** *finds another, smaller lump.*

There! Look… That's gold, yeah?

LEVI *(laughing)* You know it's gold, brother.

ENOCH If this water didn't feel so damned cold I'd think I was dreamin'.

LEVI *pulls another lump from his pan.*

LEVI It's everywhere.

ENOCH This is more gold than most men will see in a lifetime, brother.

LEVI In ten lifetimes.

ENOCH Whatever happens now, whatever we find, we split it fifty fifty. Just like I said – partners.

LEVI Partners.

ENOCH The title is in both our names, whatever the claim gives us, we share it, right down the middle.

LEVI You got a deal.

ENOCH How 'bout you sing some more of that song? You got somethin' to sing about now, brother.

LEVI You gotta sing it with me.

ENOCH You're the singer.

LEVI You know the words and the tune – ain't no one here to take offence to your tone.

> *The two brothers sing as they work. Pulling small chunks of gold from the water every now and then, laughing.*

SHE TOLD ME SHE LOVED ME
THAT SHE'D STAY BY MY SIDE,
AND IN SPRINGTIME I PROMISED
I'D MAKE HER MY BRIDE.

BUT THE WINTER WAS CRUEL,
AND HER CRUELER STILL,
BY SPRING SHE HAD LEFT ME
ALONE AND NOW ILL.

FOR THE FEVER THAT TOOK HER
HAS PUNCTURED MY HEART
AND LEFT MY LIFE BROKEN,
BATTERED AND SCARRED.

SO I'LL TO MY DARLIN'
TO STAND BY HER SIDE,
AND IN HEAVEN WE'LL MEET
THERE TO MAKE HER MY BRIDE.

Scene Three – Home

Weeks later. **ENOCH** *is lifting cases from the main room of their home when* **LEVI** *arrives.*

LEVI The first leaves are turnin'. The valley's gonna look real majestic.

ENOCH Help me with that crate.

LEVI This the last of them?

ENOCH That's it.

LEVI Have the place feelin' like home in no time. I ain't gonna miss sleepin' on the ground.

ENOCH Developin' better tastes are we, brother?

LEVI Developin' cramp in my shoulders, is all.

ENOCH Well you'll be sleepin' on the ground 'til the furniture arrives from town.

LEVI So long as I got four walls and a roof and I ain't sharing a tent with no critters.

ENOCH You found someone to come help?

LEVI I have. Miss Annelise Fischer.

ENOCH How old?

LEVI She'll be twenty one in the fall. She's been cleanin' rooms up in Black Rock 'til her brother took ill and she returned home. He passed this summer and she's been lookin' for work since.

ENOCH Good.

LEVI She'll be leavin' Eden's Croft first light the mornin' after next.

ENOCH In that case you can take care of the laundry 'til she comes. Luggin' everythin' in from the tent's got me sweatin' somethin' foul.

LEVI I'll get it done in the mornin'.

ENOCH You best take it downstream o' here. Water's running slow and I don't want to be pannin' for gold in my own juices.

LEVI It's been dry. It'll flow strong again once rains come.

ENOCH And it'll be frozen come winter.

LEVI You should be happy, brother. We've had our luck change just as you said. The claim, now the house, we've got a girl comin' to work for us, enough money to see us through.

ENOCH Yeah.

LEVI We'll get the house for ma and pa built by spring and then we'll all be together.

ENOCH Yeah.

LEVI I been thinkin' 'bout diggin' a patch out back and plantin' some vegetables. What d'you reckon? Nice fresh veggies from our own land. We could get some chickens and have eggs each day for breakfast and when they stop layin' we'll roast 'em up and have a feast.

ENOCH We ain't farmers.

LEVI I just mean enough for us.

ENOCH We have money enough to buy whatever we want. Ain't no need to slave in the mud for it.

LEVI Won't be slavin'. I'd enjoy it – workin' with my hands outdoors.

ENOCH Ain't you worked in the dirt long enough? We got plenty of money.

LEVI Not forever. What d'you reckon there is in that gold, a couple o' years?

ENOCH There's more in the claim.

LEVI What else we meant to do? Just sit around up here?

ENOCH When we need more gold we'll work the river, or we'll hire someone to work. Other than that, I'm gonna sit out on the porch with a bottle o' whiskey and enjoy every damn moment of this freedom I earned.

LEVI Well I'd go out o' my mind. I'm gonna make my plot – gonna get some seeds and get 'em planted and next summer we'll both be sat here eating hot, fresh veggies soaked in melted butter.

ENOCH You do as you please, brother.

Scene Four – Annelise Fischer

Weeks later. **LEVI** *is working in his vegetable plot. He sings as he works.*

LEVI

> CLOSE DOWN THE FIRE, SISTER,
> CLOSE THE FIRE DOWN TONIGHT.
> DAMPEN DOWN THEM FLAMES, SISTER,
> AND JUST YOU LET THEM STARS BURN BRIGHT.
>
> OH, CLOSE DOWN THE FIRE, SISTER,
> CLOSE DOWN THE FIRE NOW.
> POUR SOME WATER ON THEM FLAMES, SISTER,
> AND WON'T YOU BLESS THE ENDIN' OF THEIR
>   LIGHT.

ANNELISE That's a pretty tune.

LEVI Thank you kindly, Miss Annelise.

ANNELISE I brought out some lunch. Thought you might be hungry.

LEVI Much obliged. Has my brother eaten?

ANNELISE He's on the bottle.

LEVI What about you? Will you take lunch with me?

ANNELISE I'd be delighted.

LEVI Lunch ain't the same if you don't have no one to share it with.

ANNELISE My brother always preferred to take his alone. Said company disturbed his appetite.

LEVI I'm sorry to hear of his passin'.

ANNELISE Thank you kindly.

LEVI The two of you was close?

ANNELISE Inseparable. We was twins.

LEVI I'm sorry. Must be terrible to lose someone close.

ANNELISE He'd been ill for years 'fore it turned bad.

LEVI What was wrong with him?

ANNELISE Ain't right sure. He was born sick. His heart was weak, his bones was frail. I guess not much of him worked as it was meant to. Just chance that I was born healthy, could easily have been me was ill.

LEVI Is it wrong to say I'm glad it wasn't?

ANNELISE I don't reckon it is.

Silence.

LEVI My pa's sick.

ANNELISE Yeah?

LEVI His lungs. The cold weather makes it worse.

ANNELISE He got your ma to take care of him?

LEVI 'Til spring. Then they're gonna make the journey out here and we'll take care o' them both.

ANNELISE Enoch wants that?

LEVI More than anythin'. Breaks his heart to think of them all the way back east.

ANNELISE I thought it'd be nice to bring you out some lunch. I didn't mean for the two of us to talk only on death and disease. Tell me somethin' nice.

LEVI Like what?

ANNELISE Anythin'. Tell me somethin' nice you think about when you lie in bed at night. I mean…like a dream or somethin'.

LEVI Ever since we come here I keep havin' this dream where I got a little boy.

ANNELISE A baby?

LEVI No, grown, old enough to learn the river. I dream that we're sat by the water, and it's full of gold, like every stone is shinin' bright with gold. And it's just me and him, workin' the river, singing, with the sun on our backs.

ANNELISE That is nice.

LEVI He looks just like Enoch. Like Enoch did when he was a boy but when he sings it's in my voice. He sings better'n I ever could.

ANNELISE Is that what you want?

LEVI A son? Yeah.

ANNELISE That's real nice.

LEVI I guess I'd prefer him not to look like Enoch though. What about you? What do you want?

ANNELISE Ain't right for a girl to tell.

LEVI You can't make me tell and then you sit quiet.

ANNELISE I often think about my funeral.

LEVI Oh…

ANNELISE I know –

LEVI I thought we said no more death?

ANNELISE But it's a nice death. I'd be old, I'd have lived a good life. Most important, when all them folk are sat in the chapel thinkin' on me – I want to die knowin' I made a difference somehow, that in some way I made the world a better place.

LEVI How?

ANNELISE I ain't figured that part out yet.

LEVI Well you best get thinkin'. Ain't it your birthday next month? You're gettin' older by the day.

ANNELISE You stop it.

LEVI I'm just teasin'. Hey – you make my world a better place already.

ANNELISE Yeah?

LEVI Yeah.

Silence.

Me and my brother's too. You brought somethin' good into this valley.

ANNELISE He don't seem to think much of me.

LEVI That's just his way. Keeps his feelin's guarded from everyone. Even me sometimes.

ANNELISE I see.

LEVI My brother is burdened with an active mind. He's intelligent in his own way but he suffers days of darkness now and again. Best just to leave him to it. He'll ride it out.

ANNELISE What did the two of you do before coming out west?

LEVI We ran a store. Nothin' fancy – just sellin' general supplies. It was all Enoch really. I helped out, but he was the brains.

ANNELISE I'm sure you were invaluable.

LEVI He saved every penny he could 'til there was enough to buy the claim and travel out. Even gave up the bottle to help save. When he wants somethin' he gets real determined, ain't nothin' gonna stop him.

ANNELISE Don't seem like he wants nothin' now.

LEVI No. I guess not.

ANNELISE How long's he been like this?

LEVI Pretty much since we found the gold. You spend your whole life focussin' on gettin' somethin' or goin' somewhere and then you get it, or you get there. Once you got what you always dreamed of, that thing that's occupied your thoughts is gone, leaves an emptiness.

ANNELISE That's sad.

LEVI Don't you worry, he'll find somethin' else he wants.

ENOCH *appears from the house.*

ENOCH Ain't this cosy.

LEVI Your ears must've been burnin', brother.

ENOCH Yeah?

LEVI We was just talkin' about you.

ENOCH That right? What you sayin'?

LEVI Ain't right for a gentleman to tell.

ENOCH You ain't no gentleman, little brother.

ANNELISE He was just singin' your praises is all.

ENOCH Sings like a eunuch does our Levi. Tell me, little brother, you sportin' anythin' twixt them skinny little thighs of yours?

LEVI Enoch!

ENOCH What?

LEVI I'm sorry, Miss Annelise.

ENOCH What you sorry for, brother? You didn't say nothin' wrong did you?

LEVI You're drunk, Enoch.

ENOCH So what?

LEVI You'll make a fool of yourself.

ENOCH I don't give a damn.

LEVI You best watch your language in front of Miss Annelise.

ENOCH Miss Annelise? Don't you sound fancy. Just coz you got rich, brother, don't make you rich blooded. We're from the dirt, Miss Annelise, and you'll have to forgive our meagre ways.

ANNELISE Ain't no forgiveness needed.

ENOCH You hear that? Girl can take care o' herself. You'll excuse my brother's sensibilities, Annelise. He was too long on our mother's teat.

LEVI You should go inside and lie down.

ENOCH Not me, brother. I wish to partake in this luncheon with Miss Annelise. If she'll have me?

ANNELISE Of course.

LEVI I won't tolerate you in this state, Enoch.

ENOCH Then best you go inside and tend to your crochet or whatever gentle activity your delicate temperament might tolerate.

LEVI *stands in silence for a moment before excusing himself.*

LEVI Miss Annelise.

He is gone.

ENOCH You have sisters, Annelise?

ANNELISE No.

ENOCH Then you'll not understand the ways of brothers. We have certain behaviours with one another that might appear a little unpleasant – but it ain't that way.

ANNELISE You're old to be squabblin', ain't you?

ENOCH Nothin' to do with age. Brothers talk the same, laugh the same, fight the same from the day they were born to the day they die.

ANNELISE That so?

ENOCH Let him simmer down and we'll get along handsomely again.

Silence.

You got yourself a man, Annelise? Got yourself plans to settle down?

ANNELISE No, sir.

ENOCH What's this, 'sir'? You call me Enoch and I'll call you Annelise. That way I ain't the boss and you ain't the help – we're just two friends enjoyin' the sunshine.

ANNELISE I have work to be gettin' on with.

ENOCH Right you are. Thank you kindly for the lunch.

ANNELISE You're most welcome.

ENOCH Enoch...

ANNELISE Most welcome, Enoch.

Scene Five – A Letter From Town

LEVI *is helping* **ANNELISE** *set up for dinner.*

ANNELISE You think he'll be back in time for us to eat together? Or should I leave a bowl on the stove?

LEVI Who knows – there's a whole world of distraction in that town.

ANNELISE I'll set a place so as not to be rude if he does return.

LEVI You're always thinkin' bout keepin' folk happy. That's a real nice quality, you know?

ANNELISE Yeah?

LEVI We're all selfish – deep down we all just want what's best for ourselves. You seem to actually care about others.

ANNELISE It's just settin' out a knife and spoon.

LEVI I don't mean just this, I mean all the time. Never fails to impress me. Truth told I'm envious of that quality – wish I had a little more of it myself.

ANNELISE Ain't that selfish, to want it for yourself?

LEVI Ha! I guess so.

ANNELISE I reckon you're just fine, Levi. Don't you worry 'bout tryin' to fix yourself.

LEVI What about my brother?

ANNELISE I ain't sayin' nothin'.

LEVI He could take a leaf outta your book any day.

ANNELISE The two of you ain't nothin' alike. You know that? I'd never have picked you as brothers.

LEVI No?

ANNELISE Not just in looks, I mean in every way... Two of you like chalk and cheese.

LEVI There's reason for that.

ANNELISE Yeah? Coz he's your big brother?

LEVI No, it's more than that. He's...

ANNELISE What?

LEVI Ain't sure it's right for me to tell.

ANNELISE Please.

LEVI If he ain't said then I guess there's reason for that. I should respect it.

ANNELISE Of course.

LEVI I'm sorry, I shouldn't have said anythin' at all. It's worse to start and not finish than to just keep your mouth shut.

ANNELISE That's alright. You want a bowl of this stew?

LEVI Sounds perfect.

She prepares the food and they sit to eat.

It's nice to sit down and eat, you know. Civilised. I'm gettin' used to it after so long on the road livin' off a camp fire.

ANNELISE Must feel liberatin' though, to sit outdoors round a fire. Real simple like.

LEVI So long as you don't get eat by a grizzly. You ever camped out?

ANNELISE Can't say I have. Never crossed the country that way.

LEVI Then we'll have to do it one day. We'll take the horses and ride out 'til we don't know where we are no more. Set up a little camp, eat dinner under the stars.

ANNELISE I'd like that.

LEVI First night we came here we slept under the stars, Enoch and me. Ain't sayin' I'll give up a decent bed or food from a real kitchen – but there is somethin' to that way o' life.

ANNELISE Well I look forward to my first campin' trip, Mr Hill.

LEVI As do I, Miss Fischer.

> **LEVI** *raises his glass to toast, she does the same.* **ENOCH** *bursts in.*

ENOCH How are you toastin' when you ain't even heard the news?

LEVI Welcome back, brother.

ANNELISE Can I fix you a bowl, Enoch?

ENOCH If it's a bowl of whatever I'm smellin' I'd be mighty grateful.

LEVI You want a drink?

ENOCH What you drinkin'?

LEVI Wine.

ENOCII That'll do fine for the occasion.

LEVI What occasion? What's this news?

ENOCH All in due course, little brother.

LEVI You're lip's bleedin'.

ENOCH I ain't surprised. Took a fist to the jaw.

LEVI You deserve it?

ENOCH Why would you say such a thing? When have I ever deserved a beatin' in my life?

LEVI Who d'you aggravate?

ENOCH I paid a barman for a shot of whiskey and an empty bottle. Poured the shot down my clothes.

LEVI Yeah, I can smell.

ENOCH And so could the fellas at the card table.

LEVI I see.

ENOCH I put myself at the table with the empty bottle, squinted my eyes, slurred my words and drooped my head.

LEVI A regular pantomime.

ENOCH Placed some lousy bets and made an easy target o' myself. After a few rounds I was bone dry – all my cash gone. That's when I played the part of the prospector, in his cups for celebratin' his new wealth. I pulled out half an ounce of gold and went all in.

ANNELISE You brandished a rock of gold in a saloon? You're lucky you weren't robbed.

ENOCH The fella 'cross the table thought he was about to. Matched me, put in everythin' he has – even his fine lookin' revolver and belt.

LEVI And you win.

ENOCH Royal flush. Sucker's jaw just about hit the floor. I collect my earnin's and, while he's still scratchin' his head tryin' to figure how he lost his fortune, I drop the charade, tip my hat and in my best enunciation I thank the gentleman for his time.

ANNELISE That's when he hit you.

LEVI What happened to the winnings?

ENOCH I kept them o' course.

LEVI But you cheated.

ENOCH Oh no, brother. I did not lie, I did not play false cards – I simply offered the men some visual information from which they inferred I was unfit to play the game.

LEVI I reckon I'd have hit you myself in the circumstance.

ENOCH They're the ones tryin' to take advantage of me.

ANNELISE I'm amazed he let you take the money.

ENOCH What choice did he have? I'm the one holdin' his fine peacemaker.

He pulls the gun from beneath his coat.

LEVI So that's the news? You tricked a man of his wealth and gun?

ENOCH Oh no, little brother. The news sits inside my pocket.

He reveals a small envelope on which is written, '**ANNELISE** '.

Annelise, this here letter's for you.

ANNELISE What is it?

ENOCH Read it for yourself?

He hands it to her.

LEVI Who's it from?

ENOCH Let the girl read.

She does.

ANNELISE It's from my father.

LEVI Is everythin' alright?

She reads further.

ANNELISE Oh…

LEVI What is it?

ANNELISE He says that Mr Hill – Enoch – has asked his permission for my hand.

LEVI What?

ANNELISE My father has given his blessin'.

LEVI Enoch?

ENOCH Ain't you happy for me, brother? Ain't you happy for the two of us? Annelise is gonna be one of us for the permanent. Mrs Annelise Hill. You like the sound of that, Annelise?

ANNELISE I –

ENOCH What's your old man say?

ANNELISE He's happy I've found 'a gentleman' to take good care of me.

ENOCH Well that's it, ain't it? We'll be married 'fore the end of the month. I've made arrangements with the judge in town – just a small ceremony. What do you say, little brother?

LEVI I guess I best offer my congratulations. To the bride and groom.

ENOCH I'll drink to that!

He passes **ANNELISE** *a drink.*

To the future Mr and Mrs Enoch Hill.

They drink.

Scene Six – A Letter From The East

ENOCH *stumbles in through the door carrying* **ANNELISE**, *returning from their wedding.*

ENOCH Don't never say I ain't a gentleman.

ANNELISE I'll bear that in mind.

ENOCH Well then wife, how 'bout you bring us out a bottle?

ANNELISE Ain't you had enough?

ENOCH Worried I ain't gonna be fit to perform my conjugal duties?

ANNELISE Enoch, please.

ENOCH Ain't nothin' gonna come 'tween me and my wife tonight. Liquor or none.

ANNELISE Where's this gentleman I just been hearin' about?

ENOCH He's gonna take a momentary leave of absence.

He advances on her. **LEVI** *bursts in through the door holding a letter.*

LEVI Enoch –

ENOCH Not tonight, brother.

LEVI It's pa…

ENOCH What about him?

LEVI He's passed away. Sunday last.

Silence.

ENOCH Who's the letter from?

LEVI Mother.

ANNELISE I'm so sorry.

ENOCH What you sorry for? Old man's been dyin' long enough.

ANNELISE Even so –

ENOCH What's she said?

LEVI His lungs gave out as he slept. Says it was peaceful.

ENOCH Peaceful's a bullet in the skull, not slowly suffocatin' in your bed.

ANNELISE Enoch…

ENOCH That thought offend you, Mrs Hill? He weren't your pa.

LEVI No, he was mine.

ENOCH And mine too, brother.

ANNELISE What does this mean, for your plans?

ENOCH Means we'll bring mother out earlier than expected.

LEVI We'll send for her right away?

ENOCH I'll go myself and bring her back.

LEVI I'll go with you.

ENOCH You'll stay here.

LEVI I'd like to pay my respects to father.

ENOCH He's in the ground. You'll stay here and keep an eye on the claim.

ANNELISE I can do that.

ENOCH I am the head of this family now – you'll both do as I say.

ANA But Levi should be able to visit the grave.

ENOCH Take yourself to bed, Annelise. I'll be through in a moment.

ANNELISE But, Enoch –

ENOCH Annelise! Go…

ANNELISE Well, goodnight then. Goodnight, Levi. My condolences for your loss.

LEVI Goodnight, Annelise.

She leaves.

You don't need to talk to her like that.

ENOCH When you got a woman to talk to, you talk to her like you damn well please.

Silence.

LEVI Mother says they ran out of money. Says what pa had saved was all gone – dried up with the illness.

ENOCH Yeah?

LEVI We should have sent them somethin'– should've taken somethin' back for them.

ENOCH What's your point?

LEVI Maybe things would be different.

ENOCH Don't pin this on me.

LEVI I ain't –

ENOCH That man's been dyin' for months, ain't no gold gonna fix that.

LEVI But we should have done somethin'.

ENOCH I'm gonna do somethin' now. I'm gonna bring her here so I can take care of her like he couldn't.

LEVI Don't talk about him like that.

ENOCH Or what? What are you gonna do about it, little brother?

Silence.

Just as I thought. Like father, like son.

LEVI What does that make you?

ENOCH You watch your goddamn mouth.

There is a moment when the two could fight.

Why don't you set up that old tent and sleep outside tonight, brother.

LEVI There's gonna be a frost on the ground.

ENOCH I'm gonna head east by the end of the week. By the time I ride out I intend to have put a baby in that girl's belly. I ain't gonna make with her knowin' you're lyin' out here listen' to every sound.

LEVI I ain't sleepin' in the freezin' cold dirt. I'll rent a room in Eden's Croft, give the two of you your space. Have Annelise send for me once you're gone.

ENOCH That'd be my pleasure. You take care of yourself, little brother.

LEVI I wish you'd stop callin' me that – I'm a grown man.

ENOCH Not to me you ain't. To me you'll always be my little brother.

LEVI Give my love to ma. Tell her I'm eager to see her again. Until the new year. You travel safe.

ENOCH Goodnight, little brother.

Scene Seven – A Gift

ANNELISE *is hanging a blanket up near the fire. She sings as she works.*

ANNELISE
OH, CLOSE DOWN THE FIRE, DARLIN' SISTER,
CLOSE THE FIRE DOWN TONIGHT.
POUR SOME WATER ON THEM FLAMES,
AND BLESS THE ENDIN' OF THEIR LIGHT.

LEVI *enters the house carrying his panning tools. He joins in the song.*

BOTH
SO, WON'T YOU CLOSE DOWN THE FIRE,
CLOSE DOWN THE FIRE,
CLOSE DOWN THE FIRE NOW.
FOR THE ANGELS HANG ABOVE,
FULL OF GRACE AND FULL OF LOVE,
READY FOR TO TAKE HIS HOLY VOW.

ANNELISE You been out there late.

LEVI Sun's goin' down so early, hardly enough hours in the day.

ANNELISE Find anythin'?

LEVI Tonnes. Tonnes o' mud, water and rocks.

ANNELISE None o' them shiny rocks?

LEVI Not today.

ANNELISE Maybe you'll have better luck tomorrow.

LEVI Yeah.

ANNELISE Could be worse, couldn't it?

LEVI Always. I'm gonna wash up.

> **LEVI** *cleans his hands and face in a bowl of water.*

ANNELISE Not long 'til the new year.

LEVI That makes me sad.

ANNELISE Sad?

LEVI I don't want our time to run away.

ANNELISE *Our* time?

LEVI You know, time just moves so quick, is all. So much to get done and all the years slippin' by.

ANNELISE I see.

LEVI Speakin' of which… I got you a little somethin'.

> *He reveals a small, wrapped gift.*

ANNELISE Levi…

LEVI It is today, ain't it?

ANNELISE Yeah, but you shouldn't have.

LEVI It almost ain't nothin' – just a little somethin' to say thank you for all you've done here and, well… welcome to the family, I guess.

> *She unwraps the parcel to reveal a leather bound book.*

ANNELISE It's beautiful…

LEVI I was rememberin' how you said you wanted to make a difference in your life and – well I can't help you do it o' course – but thought you could start by writin' them things down in a nice book. Make a list o' things you wanna achieve.

ANNELISE Oh, Levi…

LEVI Could start with the new year.

ANNELISE I reckon it's just about the nicest and most thoughtful gift I've ever received.

LEVI I don't know about that.

ANNELISE Thank you.

LEVI Well… Many happy returns.

ANNELISE Hope it weren't too expensive.

LEVI Just a whole claim's worth of gold.

She smiles at him.

ANNELISE How bad is it? The claim?

LEVI Oh, ain't nothin' to worry about.

ANNELISE No, I mean it, I want to know – I'm part of this now.

LEVI Well, it ain't good. Enoch's convinced there's more out there but I ain't so sure.

ANNELISE How come?

LEVI I've worked that creek to death. Ever since we found that first strike it's been nothin' but pebbles and dirt. Reckon that might have been all the land had to offer.

ANNELISE But it was a lot you found?

LEVI Don't get me wrong, if we don't find another grain o' gold dust on this claim we'll still have been more fortunate that ninety nine in a hundred of the folk who came west for gold. I'm grateful for that at least.

ANNELISE Is it enough to last? For good, I mean?

LEVI A handful o' years at least. I worry how quick Enoch spends his share. Reckon he's capable of burnin' through it pretty fast.

ANNELISE I'll try and help with that if I can.

LEVI   Yeah, of course. You heard from him since he left?

ANNELISE   Not a word. You?

LEVI   No. And I'm not likely to neither.

ANNELISE   I hope he's alright.

LEVI   He's got his wit, ain't he? And if that should fail he's always got that six shooter.

ANNELISE   The gun?

LEVI   What?

ANNELISE   I weren't convinced he knew how to use that thing. My father always told it's more dangerous to have one you can't use than not have one at all.

LEVI   Sounds like decent advice.

ANNELISE   So I took it from his pack.

LEVI   Without him knowing?

ANNELISE   I thought that safer.

LEVI   Jesus, don't ever left him know you took it.

ANNELISE   You think I did wrong?

LEVI   I ain't sayin' that – perhaps it's best you give me the gun. I'll ride out and bury it. If he ever asks we'll both play dumb.

ANNELISE   Right.

She goes to the back room and retrieves the gun in a small wooden box.

Was I wrong in thinkin' he didn't know how to use it?

LEVI   Not entirely. Don't reckon he's ever shot a gun in his life.

A silence.

Are you happy?

ANNELISE Right now?

LEVI With him.

ANNELISE Oh…

LEVI It ain't my place to ask. I don't mean to be impertinent. Just wanna make sure you're alright.

ANNELISE What about you? You happy, Levi?

LEVI I will be.

ANNELISE When?

LEVI Don't know yet. When everythin' rights itself – when everythin' settles. Then I'll be happy.

ANNELISE Ain't it sad to be lookin' forward for happiness rather than havin' it now?

LEVI Better'n not bein' happy and not lookin' to the future for happiness neither.

ANNELISE True.

LEVI Some folk can't see how happy they should be, or what they got to be thankful for.

A long silence as **ANNELISE** *attempts to find the right words.*

I guess I best fetch in some firewood.

ANNELISE Levi…

LEVI Yeah?

ANNELISE There's been somethin' I been wantin' to ask you. But I ain't never found the words.

LEVI Yeah?

ANNELISE Perhaps I shouldn't…

LEVI Please…

ANNELISE If I'm wrong, and I might be, then please promise you'll never mention this again. I wouldn't say it if I didn't trust you'd be kind about it.

LEVI You have my word.

ANNELISE Not long after I arrived, 'bout the time of mine and Enoch's engagement, I had been feelin' somethin'. Somethin' I hoped was reciprocated. But not with Enoch.

A silence.

I might have been mistaken.

LEVI You weren't. I mean, you weren't mistaken.

ANNA Right.

LEVI The feelin's were reciprocated, as you say.

ANNELISE I see.

Another silence.

LEVI I don't know what to say.

ANNELISE I wish you'd asked my father instead of him.

LEVI I've always been afraid – I thought it must have been only in my mind.

ANNELISE I was afraid of the same thing.

LEVI Things work out how they work out – ain't nothin' we can do to alter them.

ANNELISE But I wish we –

LEVI Ain't no use in wishin'. I'm a fool for not sayin' nothin'.

A long silence.

ANNELISE Will you put your arms around me?

LEVI It ain't right, I'm sorry.

ANNELISE I can't tell you how much it hurts, whenever I'm near you I just wish you could hold me, that I could lay my head on your chest.

LEVI Please, Annelise…

ANNELISE The sufferin' of seein' you every day and knowin' I can't –

LEVI You don't need to tell me of the sufferin', Annelise. I've felt it too.

ANNELISE If you truly felt it as I do then you'd put your arms around me, lay your hands on mine. You'd kiss these lips as I have so longed to kiss yours.

LEVI But my brother…

ANNELISE He wed me with my father's blessin', but not mine…

LEVI So why d'you go through with it?

ANNELISE It just happened so fast. I didn't want it. I should have stopped it, but I didn't. I guess I hoped…

LEVI What?

ANNELISE I hoped you would stop it, that you'd say somethin' or do somethin' to show me you cared as I did for you.

LEVI I couldn't. I wish I did, but I couldn't.

ANNELISE But you can now.

Silence.

He goes to her slowly. They kiss. They embrace.

LEVI This will only bring trouble.

ANNELISE And it shall be worth it a thousand times over.

She goes to the front door.

LEVI I love you.

ANNELISE And I, you.

LEVI Where are you goin'?

ANNELISE To sit by the creek. Will you follow?

LEVI It's freezin' out.

ANNELISE Then sit by me and keep me warm.

> **LEVI** *pulls down the blanket and goes to follow her.*

> We never did get that chance to go campin' under the stars.

LEVI I guess this'll have to do.

Scene Eight – A New Home

LEVI *works the claim in the winter sun.* **ANNELISE** *brings out a cup of coffee.*

ANNELISE The water cold?

LEVI It'll be ice 'fore long.

ANNELISE I brought you a cup o' coffee.

LEVI What've I done to deserve you?

ANNELISE If the claim's run dry why d'you persevere?

LEVI I don't know. Habit.

ANNELISE Will you show me?

LEVI There ain't much to it. You scoop a selection from the creek bed, then you rock it back and forth and let all the gravel and stones tip out. If there's any gold it'll have sunk to the bottom.

ANNELISE From the weight.

LEVI As I said, ain't much to it.

Silence.

ANNELISE I been thinkin'... Once winter's over, 'fore Enoch returns, p'raps we should go.

LEVI Where?

ANNELISE Anywhere. Take your gold, head far away, start over.

LEVI I'd like that.

ANNELISE Yeah?

LEVI I ain't never felt so happy as I done with you.

ANNELISE You won't miss this place?

LEVI Course. It's been home, but we'll make a new home – just you and me.

ANNELISE What about your mother?

LEVI I'll write and explain.

ANNELISE And Enoch?

LEVI We been side by side since day I was born – I'm tired of bein' someone's little brother.

ANNELISE He'll not follow us?

LEVI I reckon he'll try. We can't leave any clues. Man could track a bear 'cross an ocean – we leave any trace he'll find us.

ANNELISE That's settled then. We wait out the winter, and we go far away.

LEVI Will you be happy then?

ANNELISE I'm happy now.

They kiss.

What d'you think, you wanna live in the city?

LEVI How come?

ANNELISE You got money now, ain't that what people want?

LEVI Not me. All them folk fightin' over the same things, over work, land, money. A man's better off kept away from all that. What d'you say to a farm?

ANNELISE Farmin' what?

LEVI Crops. Tobacco maybe.

ANNELISE Sounds perfect.

Pause.

LEVI I can't thank you enough, Annelise.

ANNELISE For what?

LEVI For speakin' when you did. For havin' the courage I didn't.

ANNELISE You're welcome.

> **LEVI** *sees something in the distance.*

LEVI Someone's comin' down the valley.

ANNELISE You make 'em out?

> *A silence as he realises.*

LEVI Get inside, Annelise.

ANNELISE What? Who is it?

LEVI Quickly. Get back inside. It's Enoch.

ANNELISE What?

LEVI Quick now.

> *She runs inside. Moments later,* **LEVI** *follows.*

Scene Nine – Enoch's Return

ENOCH *bursts in through the door – he's bloodied, brusied and covered in muck. A shotgun is strapped across his back.*

ENOCH Levi! Goddamnit, Levi!

LEVI *enters.*

LEVI Brother?

ENOCH Bring me whiskey.

LEVI Are you hurt?

ENOCH I've had worse. Where's Annelise? Annelise!

LEVI I believe she's restin'.

ENOCH Annelise! Come out here!

LEVI What happened to you?

ENOCH I was attacked.

LEVI By whom?

ANNELISE *emerges cautiously.*

ENOCH What you waitin' for, woman? Embrace your husband.

ANNELISE We weren't expectin' you 'til the spring.

LEVI Enoch, please explain.

ENOCH I was in a fight.

Silence.

Don't look at me like that, little brother. Don't you dare lay judgement on me.

ANNELISE What happened, Enoch?

ENOCH I was playin' cards…

LEVI With an empty bottle o' whiskey.

ANNELISE Oh, Jesus.

ENOCH Turns out they was the wrong fellas to play cards with.

LEVI Wrong fellas to cheat.

ANNELISE You're lucky to be alive.

ENOCH Am I? They took everythin' – my coin, my horse… my gold.

LEVI You let them take your gold?

ENOCH I didn't let nobody, they beat me near to death, left me in the horse trough to drown.

LEVI I can't believe you.

ENOCH I ain't to blame.

LEVI All you had to do was get to mother and bring her back safe. Why d'you need to try and cheat and rob along the way?

No response.

Ain't you got enough money? Ain't you rich enough?

ENOCH Not anymore. Will you bring me more whiskey?

LEVI You've had plenty.

ANNELISE *brings him another bottle.*

ANNELISE How d'you get back here?

ENOCH I went for my gun. Left it in my pack in the room I'd rented. But it was gone. Landlord had taken it – stole it.

ANNELISE You sure?

ENOCH Only time I'd left it unattended. But I'd seen he kept a shotgun 'hind the counter so I took it. Stole the shotgun and stole a horse from the livery.

LEVI They catch you for that and you'll hang.

ENOCH Lucky they didn't catch me.

LEVI Where was this?

ENOCH West Anvil.

LEVI You must have been near half way to mother. Why didn't you carry on?

ENOCH With what? If I'd got there we'd never have made it back with no coin.

LEVI So now she's left alone.

ENOCH I may be battered and weary but I've strength enough to beat you if you don't stop lookin' at me with that expression.

ANNELISE You're tired. You should rest.

ENOCH I ain't a child.

ANNELISE I'm just sayin' you need to heal these wounds. You go lie down – I'll bring some ointment.

ENOCH You're a good wife, Annelise. I've missed you.

ANNELISE And I, you. Please, Enoch, go lie down.

He gets up to leave.

ENOCH You get yourself a drink, little brother. And then you best sleep off that anger you're harborin'. I don't want to see it again.

ENOCH leaves. **ANNELISE** *and* **LEVI** *are alone for a moment. She goes to put a hand on him but he recoils. They talk in hushed tones.*

ANNELISE What do we do?

LEVI You take him the ointment like you said.

ANNELISE I mean, about us…

LEVI You don't say a word to the man. Don't even think about what's happened or he's like to see it.

ANNELISE We can still leave…

LEVI Not if he can follow. He'd find us. I need to go east and take care of my ma – you and me's gonna have to wait. I'm sorry.

ANNELISE I won't lay with him. I can't.

LEVI Then take a bottle of liquor in there and see to it he sleeps.

ANNELISE Please, Levi.

LEVI I'm sorry, Annelise.

Scene Ten – A Game Of Cards

    LEVI *and* **ANNELISE** *are sat at the table.* **ENOCH** *enters.*

ENOCH I need coffee.

LEVI That's coz last night you needed whiskey.

ENOCH What time is it?

ANNELISE It's nearly sun down.

ENOCH I slept the whole day through?

ANNELISE You've had a long journey.

ENOCH I need to talk with you, Levi.

LEVI Alright. Talk.

ENOCH Not in front of Annelise.

LEVI What you got to say that your wife can't hear?

ENOCH This is between you and me, as brothers.

ANNELISE That's fine. I'll go change the linen – that ointment's left a terrible odour.

LEVI And there I was thinkin' it was just my brother.

    ANNELISE *leaves.*

ENOCH Sit with me, Levi.

LEVI What is it you wish to discuss?

ENOCH Gold.

LEVI Yeah?

ENOCH I'm gonna need my half.

LEVI You already got your half.

ENOCH And it was taken from me.

LEVI How's that my issue?

ENOCH We're partners in this claim. We share everythin' fifty fifty. You remember?

LEVI I remember when you said you was the head of the household now. Which one is it? Are we partners or is you the boss?

ENOCH Either way, I'm gonna need my half.

LEVI You ain't gettin' it from me.

ENOCH Damn it, Levi. You can just go out to the creek and get more.

LEVI The claim's done, Enoch. There ain't no more gold.

ENOCH Course there is. Just takes work.

LEVI Why don't you work for it then?

ENOCH Coz I'm done. I'm finished. I ain't got the strength for this no more. I'm gonna take my share, take Annelise and go back home.

LEVI What happened to everythin' you wanted?

ENOCH I got everythin' I wanted, didn't I?

LEVI I guess so.

ENOCH And I want somethin' else.

LEVI What?

ENOCH I don't know yet.

LEVI When you figure it out, and you get it, what will you do then? Will you ever be content?

ENOCH Contented men die poor.

LEVI I thought you wanted to just sit out here and enjoy the view?

ENOCH I thought that too, little brother. But I sat out and looked at the view night after night and I realised I ain't meant for it.

LEVI You achieved near everythin' you ever wanted and even then find complaint.

ENOCH Guess it's in my nature.

LEVI No – I reckon a man can be what he wants to be. It ain't set in stone. Does Annelise want to go with you?

ENOCH She's my wife, ain't she? She'll follow where I go.

LEVI I ain't givin' you my gold.

ENOCH You know I always get what I want, brother.

LEVI That right?

ENOCH I'll play you for it.

LEVI What?

ENOCH A game of cards.

LEVI You ain't got nothin' to bet with.

ENOCH My share of the claim.

LEVI The claim's worthless.

ENOCH What d'you want?

LEVI You ain't got nothin' I want.

> **ENOCH** *chuckles to himself.*

ENOCH I beg to differ, little brother. Annelise, come out here.

LEVI What are you doin'?

ENOCH I got somethin' you want alright. Annelise!

LEVI Stop it.

ENOCH I seen the way you look at her. Ever since the day she arrived you been droolin' over the girl like a drunk in the saloon.

ANNELISE *emerges.*

LEVI I ain't playin' this game.

ANNELISE What's goin' on?

ENOCH Just got ourselves a little wager, is all.

LEVI Can you hear yourself, Enoch? This ain't no whisky takin' – this is you. You hear what you become?

ENOCH Come here, Annelise.

LEVI I ain't no drunk at the bar you can try and play your tricks on.

ENOCH Me and Levi is gonna have ourselves a game of poker. I win, he gives me half his stash o' gold. I lose, and he gets a taste of somethin' not even all that gold can buy.

ANNELISE What you talkin' about, Enoch?

ENOCH Take a look at that prize, little brother. Don't tell me you don't want her stink all over you.

ANNELISE Enoch! Don't speak like that.

ENOCH You're my wife, damn it. I'll speak however I please.

ANNELISE I ain't toleratin' this –

ANNELISE *goes to leave but* ENOCH *lunges for her.* LEVI *forces his way between them.*

LEVI You get your goddamn hands off her. You don't ever touch her again.

A moment of realisation from ENOCH. *He laughs manically.*

ENOCH   Little brother! You think you're the man of the house now? Huh?

ANNELISE   Enoch…

ENOCH   Think coz I been away a few weeks you can strut round here like a damn peacock?

ANNELISE   Please…

ENOCH   You think you can defend my wife's honor, from me?

ANNELISE   He weren't –

ENOCH   Huh?

> *Silence.*

You fallen for her, ain't you?

> *Silence.*

What about you, Annelise? How d'you feel about my little brother?

> *Silence.*

Now you shut up – I asked you how you felt.

> *Pause.*

ANNELISE   I love him.

> **ENOCH** *laughs slowly.*

ENOCH   Jesus fucking Christ…

ANNELISE   I'm sorry…

ENOCH   What you gone and done, little brother?

ANNELISE   It weren't him, Enoch. It were me.

LEVI   It were the both of us.

ENOCH I ain't surprised by some fickle whore, Levi. But you? You're my brother. You're my brother and you betrayed me.

LEVI You betrayed yourself when you became the man you are.

ENOCH I've become the man I was born to be.

LEVI I hardly recognise you anymore. Ever since we found that gold, I ain't seen my brother when I looked at you.

ENOCH Recognise me or not, you betrayed me, and I'm still your brother.

LEVI No. My brother died long ago.

ENOCH I share your sorrow. For mine is about to.

> **ENOCH** *goes for the shotgun.* **ANNELISE** *dives forward and tries to stop him.*

ANNELISE Levi, run!

> **LEVI** *darts out the door.* **ENOCH** *wrestles* **ANNELISE** *from the gun, holding her by the throat and forcing her to the ground. He releases her and heads out the door. She chokes and splutters.*

ANNELISE Enoch! Don't!

Epilogue – By The Light of a Blood Red Moon

In the Chapel of Emmanuel, LEVI *is confessing to* FATHER MANOAH.

LEVI Before the sun is up, I will take my brother's life, or I'll die in the endeavour.

MANOAH Why?

LEVI He will follow me here. And he'll attempt to take mine.

MANOAH Surely he can be reasoned with?

LEVI Ain't no reason left to him. I have no choice.

MANOAH You must find another path. If you cannot reason with him you must flee.

LEVI I won't leave Annelise behind.

MANOAH She's not yours to protect.

LEVI You don't understand him, father.

MANOAH Perhaps tonight I'll get the chance.

LEVI You must take yourself away from here. Get out of danger.

MANOAH I beg you to reconsider.

LEVI I'm sorry father. I know what I must do.

> **LEVI** *pulls the wooden box from his pack and removes the gun.*

MANOAH Someone's approaching.

LEVI Hide yourself, father.

MANOAH I have nothing to fear.

LEVI So be it.

The doors swing open. **ENOCH** *enters, armed with the shotgun.*

ENOCH I should have known you'd come here.

LEVI Where's Annelise?

ENOCH Where you left her.

LEVI You hurt her?

ENOCH You think I'd harm my own wife?

LEVI The priest wants me to reason with you, Enoch.

ENOCH That so? Then how come you're holdin' my gun?

Silence.

You steel that from me 'fore I left? You wanted me to get in trouble out there and never return?

LEVI Of course not.

ENOCH You confess all your sins, little brother? You tell the padre how you made a cuckold of your own brother?

LEVI That weren't my intent.

ENOCH The girl's mine, Levi.

LEVI I did you wrong, I know that. But you always knew I cared for her. Tell me it ain't true that's the reason you wanted her for yourself.

ENOCH I won her fair.

LEVI She ain't somethin' to be won. If you understood her as I have come to –

ENOCH Don't talk to me of my own wife. You hearin' all this confession, father?

MANOAH I am hearing two brothers torn in anger. But that tear is reparable. This can be resolved.

ENOCH Damn right it can – when one of us hits the dirt.

MANOAH I don't believe you would harm your brother.

>   **ENOCH** *laughs slowly.*

ENOCH This dude ain't my brother. Didn't he tell you that, father? Ain't you told the whole story, Levi?

LEVI We share a mother.

MANOAH That makes you brothers.

ENOCH Not in our mother's eyes it didn't. She ain't never looked at me like she looked at her sweet little Levi.

LEVI Coz she feared you'd turn out bad. She worried you'd become the man you have. It'd break her heart to see you now.

ENOCH Say it, brother. Say what you mean. Coz she feared I'd turn out to be like my father.

LEVI Haven't you?

ENOCH You see, padre. Levi's old man, the man who raised us both, he ain't my daddy.

LEVI He raised you as his own son.

ENOCH But ma was right, weren't she. Don't matter how a boy's raised – it's what's in his blood that counts. Turns out I got the blood of a vicious, murderin', son of a bitch rapist.

LEVI You've chose to be the man you are, Enoch. You can't blame that on no one but yourself.

ENOCH The man who sired me swung from a rope not twelve months from my birth. He murdered a county judge and they hanged him for it. That's the poison that runs in my veins.

MANOAH This can be resolved without murder.

ENOCH Death resolves all, father.

LEVI We came out here as brothers – to find our fortune together. Ever since we found that gold it's done nothin' but tear us apart. Your dreams came true and you gave up on livin'.

LEVI *pulls a coin bag from his coat and drops it on the altar.*

That's it. That's the gold. More than a man could need. You willin' to die for it?

ENOCH Are you?

LEVI No. Not for gold – for Annelise.

ENOCH Then there we have it. Both of us's gonna fight for that girl. Fighting for the love of a woman – a noble way to die.

A long silence.

MANOAH Enoch, Levi, you don't have to die here.

LEVI One of us does.

ENOCH You ready, little brother?

LEVI *nods and takes position.*

A long silence.

Goodnight, little brother.

ENOCH *goes to fire but a shot rings out before he has the chance.* **ANNELISE** *stands in the doorway, a smoking revolver in her hand.* **ENOCH** *hits the ground, dead.*

LEVI Annelise?

ANNELISE As the priest says, the two of you was brothers.

Ain't right for you to take his life. But I ain't gonna let him kill you neither.

LEVI Are you harmed?

ANNELISE Unlike you pair, my father taught me how to shoot this thing. He made me pack it when I travelled to your claim in case one of you wasn't honorable.

LEVI He's a wise man.

> **LEVI** *goes to her. She stops him with the gun.*

Annelise?

ANNELISE Don't come no closer.

LEVI What are you doin'?

ANNELISE I have to ask forgiveness, father. I hoped when I followed Enoch here tonight I'd have the chance to end this all – to take his life. I'm afraid now, if what he says is true, then I must take two more.

MANOAH Please, child, do not act rashly.

ANNELISE The poisoned blood that ran in his veins, it now runs in mine and the child that grows within me.

LEVI No...

ANNELISE I heard what Enoch said.

LEVI I know you're afraid but you have to trust me, Annelise. Enoch made himself that way. Weren't nothin' to do with his blood. Ain't that right, father?

MANOAH I believe we all choose our paths in this life. The man you are born to be is not the man you must become.

ANNELISE I can't raise a child and watch him turn out like Enoch.

LEVI You won't have to. I'll raise the child with you. We'll never say a word of Enoch. The child will never know the truth; he'll just know his mother, and his father. I'll love him as my own son, we'll travel back east to my mother and we'll start a new life for ourselves far away from all this – just like we planned.

MANOAH Please, Annelise. Enough blood has been spilled this night. Levi offers hope, he offers this child a chance – you must take it.

ANNELISE *slowly lowers the gun.*

ANNELISE I can't live to be afeared of my own child.

LEVI I ain't gonna let no harm come to you or that baby. We're family now.

MANOAH Listen to him, Annelise, he means well for you both.

ANNELISE *(to* LEVI*)* Are you sure?

LEVI I ain't never been so certain of anythin' in my life.

LEVI *goes to her. They embrace.*

Father Manoah, I'm sorry to bring this sufferin' to your house. If the law men come, what will you tell them?

MANOAH That I didn't see anything.

LEVI Thank you, father.

MANOAH You'll be wanting your gold back?

LEVI *looks to* ENOCH*'s body.*

LEVI Half.

ANNELISE Levi?

LEVI Use the other half to pay for a decent burial for my brother. I want him buried in a tailored suit, in a decent coffin.

MANOAH Of course. And a marking on the grave?

LEVI Enoch Hill. No inscription.

MANOAH Very well.

LEVI They'll be money enough left to feed a family for near two years. You keep it – put it to the church, give it to those in need.

MANOAH That's most generous.

LEVI I pray it brings you better fortune than it did my brother.

> **LEVI** *collects the shotgun from the floor and lays it on the altar with the revolver. He collects half the gold.*

These guns is worth decent coin. You sell them, you bury them – do what you like. We've no more need for them.

MANOAH You should stay here until the sun rises.

LEVI The moon's glowin' strong enough for us to see by. I want all of this behind us come the light of day.

MANOAH I understand. Before you leave, you should say a few words for your brother.

LEVI A prayer? Enoch wouldn't have wanted that.

MANOAH A farewell then.

> **LEVI** *lowers himself to* **ENOCH**'*s body, removes his hat and holds it to his heart. He places a hand on his brother.*

LEVI For all you did for me, thank you. I hope that wherever you are now, that you might have finally found peace.

> **LEVI** *stands, replaces his hat and moves to the door with* **ANNELISE**. *He takes one final look at the chapel and, at its center,* **ENOCH**.

Goodnight, big brother.

The End

The Frontier Trilogy: Volume II

The Clock Strikes Noon

CHARACTERS

BENJAMIN 'BEN' WALKER – A farmer, running for sheriff. 30-40. He is calm, confident, and strong. He is a natural leader who easily commands the respect of those around him.

SHERIFF FELIX JACKSON – A lawman and farm owner. 30-40. Crippled with paranoia and insecurity, he is defensive and relentlessly hostile.

LILLIAN 'MISS LILY' DAVENPORT – Daughter of COLONEL DAVENPORT, head of the American Pacific Railroad. 25-35. She is calm, level-headed and aggressively well spoken. She hides her true nature beneath a veneer of polite civility.

FATHER MANOAH – The priest at The Chapel of Emmanuel. 30-40. He is powerful and has a gravity that demands men listen to his words.

SETTING

The Chapel of Emmanuel, North of Canyon Falls, America

Spring 1864

The glow of a late morning sun fills the Chapel of Emmanuel. Gunshots are heard in the near distance.

The chapel doors fly open and two armed men burst in, immediately slamming the doors closed behind them and pinning them shut.

BENJAMIN WALKER *is stocky, strong jawed and handsome; he has the look of a man who works outdoors.* **FELIX JACKSON**, *by comparison, appears weak and pale; a 'tin star' is pinned to his chest.*

BENJAMIN Check the back!

FELIX *(calling out)* There anyone here?

A voice comes from the back room.

MANOAH *(off)* Who's out there?

FELIX We're armed. Don't come out shootin'! Come out slow, hands up to the sky.

MANOAH *(off)* I'm the priest. I'll not be held hostage in my own church.

FELIX How'd I know you's the priest? You'll come out with your hands to the sky or I'll be quick with this trigger.

BENJAMIN It's alright, father, we ain't gonna shoot. You just need to come out slow so my friend here don't lose his nerve.

FELIX Walker?

BENJAMIN You ain't gonna shoot no priest.

FELIX He could be one o' them!

BENJAMIN I know the man.

MANOAH *(off)* Is that you, Benjamin?

BENJAMIN Yes, father. It's alright – you come out slow.

> *Slowly, the rear door of the chapel opens. Out steps* **FATHER MANOAH**, *his eyes covered with a black bandage. He is blind.*

Father Manoah, we're in trouble.

MANOAH So it would seem.

FELIX What's out through that door? That one you come from.

MANOAH My quarters.

FELIX You got a back door out of this place?

MANOAH It's my private quarters.

FELIX I don't give a damn! I ain't messin' here, padre. Answer the damn question.

MANOAH Who is this man, Benjamin?

FELIX Who cares? I'm holdin' a gun ain't I?

BENJAMIN It's Sheriff Jackson, father.

MANOAH You don't sound like a law man.

FELIX Is there a goddamn way out o' this church?

BENJAMIN Please, father…

MANOAH There's a door. Leads out to the east.

FELIX You stay here, I'm gonna check it.

> **FELIX** *rushes out.*

BENJAMIN Thank you, father. You should stay low – keep away from them windows. I'm sorry to bring this trouble here.

MANOAH What trouble are you in, son?

BENJAMIN The kind that gets you into your six by three.

FELIX *returns.*

FELIX Ain't no good – they already got at least two men up on the ridge.

BENJAMIN Right. You locked the door?

FELIX And shuttered the windows.

BENJAMIN Help me with this bar here.

The two men lift a wooden bar across the chapel doors, sealing them in.

FELIX What if they torch the place?

MANOAH It's a church, son. Who are these men you've so angered they might set alight a house of God?

BENJAMIN They ain't gonna burn it down.

FELIX They burnt everythin' else.

BENJAMIN All the same, father, p'raps it's best we get you out.

MANOAH I won't flee my own church.

FELIX Well don't say we ain't warned you.

BENJAMIN We need to know everythin' 'bout your chapel, father. Is there any other way they could get in?

MANOAH Only the two doors – both of which you've sealed.

FELIX You got any weapons in here? Anythin' we can use?

MANOAH I beg your pardon?

FELIX Firearms, padre. Guns…

MANOAH This is a house of God.

FELIX Save takin' offence for when they storm this place and we ain't got enough firepower.

MANOAH It's been many years since a man talked to me like you're doin', son.

FELIX Well don't take it personal.

MANOAH I can tell you're not a God fearing man.

FELIX I'm a man fearin' man, padre. Man with a gun's somethin' to be afeared of.

MANOAH I disagree, Sheriff. A man with a gun is but a mortal fear – the fear of God is eternal.

FELIX Save the sermon, padre.

MANOAH There was a time when someone spoke to me like that they'd soon come to regret it.

BENJAMIN I'm sorry, father. He don't mean nothin' by it. Do you, Felix?

FELIX Yeah I don't mean nothin' by it.

BENJAMIN We're safe in here for the time bein'. But fact is we're surrounded. Only way out is through the doors and they got guns aimed on 'em.

FELIX Only way out is to shoot our way out, I guess.

BENJAMIN Them's trained men out there – killers. I'm a half decent shot but I ain't nothin' up against men like that.

FELIX I reckon I'd give 'em a run for their money.

BENJAMIN You reckon? I reckon I saw your shootin' back there and I'm lucky to be alive the way you was takin' pot shots out into the brush.

FELIX I could shoot a man from a hundred yards on horseback. You make the same claim?

BENJAMIN Why not, for all yours is worth I can shoot the same man from a thousand.

FELIX Bullshit.

BENJAMIN Watch your mouth – you ain't proppin' up the saloon bar, Sheriff.

BENJAMIN *looks through a shutter in the main chapel doors.*

There's a few of them convening up by the tracks to the west.

FELIX How many?

BENJAMIN Looks to be less than half a dozen. How many you see out back?

FELIX Just the two, I saw. What d'we do now?

BENJAMIN You're the law man, you tell me.

FELIX My idea was to come in here. That's kept us alive this long. I ain't gotta come up with all the damn plans.

BENJAMIN We ain't gonna walk out. They ain't gonna ride in. So we wait.

FELIX I should have deputised a posse. I should have seen this comin' a mile off.

BENJAMIN Why didn't you?

FELIX This ain't the election campaign, Walker – you got a problem with how I'm dealin' with things you keep it to yourself. We gotta wait in here for the rest of our short lives I don't wanna have to hear your voice ringin' in my ears.

BENJAMIN We should check our weapons. We gotta wait we may as well be ready for when they come.

They check their guns. **FELIX** *carries a long barrelled revolver.* **BENJAMIN** *is armed with a peacemaker and a repeater rifle.*

FELIX I got one shot left.

BENJAMIN You ain't got no spares?

FELIX I weren't anticipatin' a god damn fire fight 'fore lunch.

BENJAMIN Two rounds in the repeater. I got enough to make up a full six in the forty-four.

FELIX Nine bullets… I'll just send a telegram up to the fort. 'Don't worry about it fellas, we got nine bullets and only 'bout half a dozen shooters to dispatch. You stay in and put your feet up – we'll be just fine.'

BENJAMIN So long as we use 'em right, nine shots'll be plenty.

FELIX You sure you ain't got a gun, padre?

MANOAH There are no weapons here.

FELIX Maybe there is and you ain't seen 'em. Maybe you been eatin' your dinner with a peacemaker for a spoon and you just ain't realised.

MANOAH Your attempt at humour is misguided, Sheriff.

FELIX That so?

BENJAMIN Leave it, Felix.

MANOAH You've come in here, Benjamin, you'd put me in danger, put the church at risk – I deserve an explanation.

FELIX Coz we were gettin' shot at.

MANOAH I asked Benjamin.

FELIX You want an explanation, didn't you?

BENJAMIN They're from the American Pacific, father. They're Davenport's men – railroad men.

MANOAH Why the violence?

BENJAMIN Every settler, homesteader and farmer with land 'tween the Eastern Canyon and Cooper's Ridge have been approached by Davenport's representatives tryin' to force 'em out.

MANOAH I see.

BENJAMIN Started peaceful – deals, offers, lawyers. But ain't no one 'bout to give up their homes for the sake of AP saving a few dollars on track. As their road got closer they got more and more forceful 'til this mornin', they started burnin' crop.

FELIX They ran out two hundred head of cattle from my land. Butchered near ten o' them.

BENJAMIN They got vicious, tryin' to force us, scare us into leavin'. Few of us tried to run 'em off. That's when it turned violent.

FELIX Was them started shootin' first, padre. Make note of that for when I'm standing before St Peter.

MANOAH Where are your families?

FELIX Ain't got none.

MANOAH Benjamin, your children?

BENJAMIN They're safe. Caroline met with the other women and they're headin' to town 'til this settles.

MANOAH And the other men? The other farmers who rode out with you?

FELIX Dead.

MANOAH How many?

BENJAMIN Three. All three of them family men.

MANOAH I'm sorry.

BENJAMIN Good men who didn't deserve to die over no piece of land.

MANOAH No man deserves to die over land, Benjamin.

FELIX But we ain't defenceless, neither. I took down one of theirs. Shot right in the gut, watched him hit the dirt behind us.

MANOAH It's not right to relish in a man's demise, Sheriff.

FELIX Is when he's tryin' to bring about yours, padre.

> **BENJAMIN** *is looking through the shutter on the door again.*

BENJAMIN I can make out five. With your two that makes seven.

FELIX How many d'you say there was to start with?

BENJAMIN I counted a dozen.

FELIX With the one I shot that means there's at least another four out there unaccounted for.

BENJAMIN Just the one.

FELIX What?

BENJAMIN There's two out back, five out front, one unaccounted for, one you shot and the three I shot.

FELIX Bull…

BENJAMIN I ain't got no cause to be makin' up stories.

FELIX You're tryin' to make out you're a better shot that me.

BENJAMIN I ain't interested in campaign politics, Felix. I'm tellin' you I shot three, you shot one, so there's four of them dead and one out there somewhere we can't see 'im.

FELIX Next you'll be sayin' how each one o' them shots was straight to the head.

BENJAMIN I didn't leave 'em on the ground to die from no gut shot that's for certain.

> *A sharp whistle sounds in the distance. A steam locomotive pulls itself to a stop near the chapel.*

> **BENJAMIN** *looks back through the shutter.*

FELIX What is it?

BENJAMIN What d'you think it is?

FELIX Why they brought in a train for?

BENJAMIN Reinforcements.

FELIX Seven against two, they ain't happy with their odds?

BENJAMIN We're protected, and we got a clean line of sight for at least two hundred yards in every direction. It ain't just about numbers.

FELIX Why do I always feel like you're tryin' to educate me, Walker?

BENJAMIN Maybe coz you feel dumb in my presence.

MANOAH The two of you have enough to your concern without turning on each other.

BENJAMIN Sheriff Jackson and I have been fierce competitors for some time, father.

MANOAH Is that so?

FELIX He's been running for my position is what's so.

MANOAH Sheriff Benjamin Walker?

BENJAMIN Not that it matters now. We get out of this alive we can start back to squabblin' over politics.

Back at the shutter.

At least ten come off the train.

FELIX You reckon Davenport's out there?

BENJAMIN From what I heard the man don't deal with his own problems – hides behind all manner of folk 'fore he'll get his hands dirty.

FELIX If there's near fifteen of them to the west I'm guessin' we'd be better off with the two out east.

BENJAMIN You want to make a run for it?

FELIX The odds are only gettin' worse by the minute.

BENJAMIN What about the one unaccounted for?

FELIX What about him?

BENJAMIN He could be hidden right outside with a two-gauge pointed at the door.

FELIX Or he could be on the other side of the tracks takin' a dump.

BENJAMIN It's a gamble.

FELIX Ain't you a gamblin' man?

BENJAMIN Not with my own life.

FELIX What if we take the pastor with us? What if we threaten like we're gonna shoot him?

BENJAMIN What?

MANOAH I'll not go easily, Sheriff.

BENJAMIN We ain't harmin' the priest, Felix.

FELIX I ain't sayin' we harm him, just give them out there the impression we will.

BENJAMIN Everythin' we do today, everythin' we done, we done right. If we're gonna die we ain't gonna die like cowards with a gun to the priest's head.

FELIX It were just an idea.

BENJAMIN Well you keep them ideas to yourself in future.

FELIX I am a law man, and elected law official – you're just a god damn farmer. You don't speak for me.

BENJAMIN I ain't tryin' to speak for you. I just wish you'd stop speakin' for yourself.

FELIX I ain't never been to church, Walker. I ain't gonna die in one. If I'm gonna die I wanna die with whiskey in my belly in a crowded street – not like some rat in a hole.

BENJAMIN You wanna go out there you be my guest. But I'm stayin' put.

FELIX You're a fool.

BENJAMIN You walk out there and you'll be a dead fool. Or if you don't die, you make it back to town, what then? What you gonna tell the folk in town, you ran away leavin' the priest and a farmer to do your job?

The train lets out another long whistle and its engines come to life. **BENJAMIN** *rushes to the shutter.*

It's leavin'. The train's headin' back down the tracks.

FELIX They givin' up?

BENJAMIN The men ain't goin' with it.

MANOAH Perhaps it would be a good time to say a prayer?

FELIX I ain't never prayed – I ain't startin' now.

BENJAMIN Perhaps you can say a prayer for us, father? I'd be grateful for that.

FELIX I'd be grateful for some of that sacramental wine I hear so much about.

MANOAH There is no wine here.

FELIX You don't even keep a bottle of whiskey for your own medicinal purposes?

MANOAH From what I hear, Sheriff, you aren't the best shot with that pistol – seems to me like liquor is only gonna discourage your aim.

FELIX How d'you know, padre? You ever shot a gun? You know what it feels like to kill a man?

BENJAMIN Someone's comin'…

FELIX What?

BENJAMIN From the train. Someone's comin'.

BENJAMIN *grabs the rifle and takes aim through the shutter.*

Go keep watch from the back. They might be tryin' to distract us.

FELIX *goes out the back.* **BENJAMIN** *cocks the lever on the rifle.*

MANOAH Don't shoot yet, Benjamin. There's no harm in holding fire 'til he gets closer.

BENJAMIN You sure you're blind, father?

MANOAH I know the sound of a repeater being cocked. Just wait 'til the man is close enough to call out. There may be a peaceful way out of this for the two of you after all.

BENJAMIN It's a woman…

MANOAH What?

BENJAMIN Comin' down from the train, it's a woman. Felix! Come back through.

FELIX *emerges.*

It's a woman, she's wavin' a white handkerchief.

FELIX You reckon it's a trick?

BENJAMIN You see anythin' out back?

FELIX The two men's still up on the ridge.

BENJAMIN I reckon this woman might just want to talk. I reckon I might just let her.

FELIX Don't take your gun offa her.

BENJAMIN She comes under a sign of truce, Felix. Keep your gun to hand but don't raise it at her or we'll likely find ourselves in far deeper water.

Lowering his weapon he calls out through the shutter.

Don't come no closer.

LILLIAN *(off)* I'm here to talk. I ain't armed.

BENJAMIN I got your word there ain't no one gonna try and storm in here?

LILLIAN *(off)* I've just come to talk, there's nothing funny going on here. You have my word.

FELIX *(quietly)* The word of a woman – what's that worth?

LILLIAN *(off)* Do I have yours that you won't do nothing stupid?

BENJAMIN We have guns.

LILLIAN *(off)* I'd expect that. You gonna use them?

BENJAMIN Not if we ain't given cause.

LILLIAN *(off)* You'll get no cause from me.

BENJAMIN Then you have my word.

LILLIAN *(off)* What about your friend in there?

BENJAMIN *(whispered)* Go on…

FELIX You have mine also.

LILLIAN *(off)* Anyone else in there?

BENJAMIN Just the priest, he ain't armed and he ain't lookin' to involve himself.

LILLIAN *(off)* Very well. You best open the doors, step away and I'll come inside.

The two men look at each other before lifting the wooden bar from the door.

BENJAMIN *opens the doors and the two men retreat into the chapel, guns at their sides.*

>   LILLIAN DAVENPORT *enters. She is young and clearly*
>   *wealthy; her dress, hair and mannerisms appear out of*
>   *place in this setting. She closes the doors behind her.*

Good morning, gentleman. Good morning, father.

MANOAH Good morning.

BENJAMIN You got a name for us?

LILLIAN Lillian Davenport, you may call me Lillian or Miss
Lily.

FELIX Davenport? Your pa sent you down here?

LILLIAN I'm here at the request of my father who wishes
me to resolve this situation as quickly as is possible.

FELIX Man sends woman to do his talkin'? This what we've
been runnin' from?

LILLIAN Let me start by informing you two gentlemen
that I have a highly skilled individual positioned to
the north of this building. I'm not acquainted with
the technical apparatus in which he is so highly skilled
as to do it justice, but let me tell it to you as he did
to me. This individual possesses a lensed rifle that
enables him to shoot a man at near a thousand yards
with accuracy enough to render that man infertile. If
anyone walks out of this building before me, you won't
make two feet 'fore he cuts you down. Am I clear?

BENJAMIN Perfectly.

>   LILLIAN *reveals a pocket watch and checks the time.*

LILLIAN Excellent. Let me also inform you that the time
is a quarter to twelve midday. Are both you gentlemen
aware of the station clock recently installed at Whistle
Point?

BENJAMIN I am.

FELIX Yeah.

LILLIAN It's a magnificent feat of engineering, uses the power of the wind to keep it alive. It'll never die, so long as the wind keeps blowing. Isn't that marvellous.

BENJAMIN I don't follow your meanin'.

LILLIAN When that clock chimes twelve, my father, Colonel Davenport, the owner and Chief Executive of the American Pacific Railroad will be collected in his private car by the train that departed St Emmanuel's not five minutes ago. That train will bring him here. Can you guess at the purpose of his journey to this church?

BENJAMIN He want to confess his sins?

LILLIAN Ha! What a wicked sense of humour you have, sir. No, he is coming to this church to collect the signed contracts made between the APR and the two of you gentlemen.

FELIX What contracts? I ain't signed no contract.

LILLIAN Of course you haven't, Mr Jackson. They are here in my possession.

She reveals two contracts.

I have come to collect your signatures, so that when my father arrives he does not have to.

BENJAMIN What gives you the impression we're gonna sign them?

LILLIAN Call it... intuition, Mr... Well, how rude of me, I have not asked your name.

BENJAMIN But you know his.

LILLIAN The tin star on his chest – I made an educated guess that this gentleman is Sheriff Jackson.

BENJAMIN My name is Benjamin Walker.

LILLIAN The leaseholder of Blackwater?

BENJAMIN I'm the owner of that farm.

LILLIAN Of course.

BENJAMIN So, Miss Lily, what play you gonna make to get us to sign them papers?

LILLIAN It's no play, Mr Walker. I have a fine offer for the titles of both your properties. I'm authorised by my father in this here telegram to pay you handsomely for your troubles.

BENJAMIN Troubles? What of the crop your burned, the cattle slaughtered? What about the three men who died out here today at the hands of your railroad thugs?

LILLIAN I have been informed of the death of your neighbours. It grieves me it truly does. But I have also been informed that it was you who rode out for the APR men. Is that not true? Is it not true that the two of you men took the lives of four of the APR's? One of whom is suffering slowly from a bullet to his abdomen.

BENJAMIN Those men burned our crops and ruined our livelihoods.

LILLIAN That's business, Mr Walker. Not the kind of business you folk might be accustomed to but it's big business. It's how big business get's done. In these documents you'll see you are beyond reimbursed for the losses you have suffered.

BENJAMIN We all turned down your offers before. I turned it down. What makes you think anythin's changed?

LILLIAN With all due respect, Mr Walker, everything's changed.

BENJAMIN Coz you got us cornered? Coz you got us under the watch of your rifleman?

LILLIAN He's not there to persuade you, Mr Walker. That's my job. He's out there to protect me so I am able to do my job.

BENJAMIN Well then, be my guest.

LILLIAN Would you mind, before I speak, I'd be eternally grateful for a glass of water.

BENJAMIN Father Manoah, would you provide this for the lady?

MANOAH Of course.

MANOAH goes out the back.

LILLIAN I find it awful dry out here. I spent much of my youth in Mississippi where the heat clings to you in moisture. Some find that suffocating, not me. I find the dryness of your deserts to be far more affecting, it tires me – even in spring. Until recently I have spent my years in the capital city of Washington D.C. where my father is based. Or was until his ventures with the railroad brought him out west.

MANOAH returns with a glass of water.

Thank you, father.

She drinks.

My, that is fresh. Tell me, have you ever been to Washington D.C., Mr Walker?

BENJAMIN I have not.

LILLIAN The City of New York?

BENJAMIN No.

LILLIAN Well you must. And when the American Pacific Railroad is complete you'll be able to with such ease. This railroad will connect the two sides of our great continent and transform the west for the better.

BENJAMIN What if we don't want the west transformin'?

LILLIAN It's already happened. It's happening with every breath. It's like a wave, Mr Walker, a wave heading across this barren land saturating it, nourishing it. If you stand in its way you'll be knocked to the ground. But if you ride with it, Mr Walker, that wave will journey you further than you'd imagined.

BENJAMIN You practised that speech?

LILLIAN I'm talking about progress, Mr Walker. I'm talking about what the American Pacific is going to bring to people like yourself.

BENJAMIN So far it's just brought pain and sufferin'.

LILLIAN To a great many, I won't dispute that. I myself have suffered the toil of helping to bring these rails across the continent.

BENJAMIN Toil? You ever raised a hammer, Miss Lily? You ever worked the ground?

LILLIAN There are many kinds of toil, Mr Walker. You'll see that for yourself when the APR is complete. The opportunities for ordinary working men like yourself. We are entering a new era, Mr Walker. The future is for men like you, men who want more than what they're born with.

BENJAMIN That's the man you think I am?

LILLIAN Am I wrong?

He smiles.

We need your land in order to make the Pacific. We can't build our road in the sky, Mr Walker.

BENJAMIN There are many ways to the Pacific, Miss Lily. Why can't you go around? Find someone willing to sell?

LILLIAN We have deadlines. We have costs to consider. The costs of rerouting to the south, not to mention the additional time required, are beyond consideration, Mr Walker.

BENJAMIN So you pay us double our land's worth, and compensation, in these here documents, and even then APR's still makin' a tidy savin'?

LILLIAN As I said, Mr Walker, big business.

BENJAMIN We're folk who ain't so fond of big business, we like it the old fashioned way. I like to look a man in the eyes when I make a deal, I like to be able to shake his hand.

LILLIAN When my father arrives you'll be able to shake his hand if that'll ease your soul, Mr Walker.

BENJAMIN He lets you speak for him?

LILLIAN He does. But let me tell you that I speak with far more patience than my father. He's not a man folk say no to, Mr Walker.

BENJAMIN What if we refuse to sign?

LILLIAN I'm not gonna make threats. You're an intelligent man, I'm sure you understand the potential consequences here.

BENJAMIN What's to stop you gettin' the contracts signed and shootin' us anyhow?

LILLIAN You'll have my word, Mr Walker. Though I am a woman, the word of a Davenport is considered binding above all else.

She hands over the pocket watch.

Gentlemen, it's five to twelve. I'm going to leave this pocket watch here with you, Mr Walker, and I'm gonna step outside and take in the cool midday sun. Give you gentlemen a few minutes to speak your minds freely.

When the clock strikes noon, Mr Walker, my father will be on his way, and I'll expect your decision. I'll step outside.

She goes to the door.

You know, Mr Walker, that watch is worth near two hundred American dollars. It was a gift from the President to my father. You sign them papers, and I'll let you keep it. Gentlemen.

She leaves.

The men bar the doors again. **BENJAMIN** *checks through the shutter to make sure she is beyond earshot.*

BENJAMIN Felix, you should check the back again, make sure they ain't crept up while we was talkin'.

FELIX Right.

> **FELIX** *goes out the back.*

MANOAH You don't trust her?

BENJAMIN Would you?

MANOAH Perhaps not.

BENJAMIN She says she wants a peaceful resolve – I fear it may be too late for that.

> **FELIX** *returns.*

FELIX So we gonna sign?

BENJAMIN You want to?

FELIX I don't wanna die.

BENJAMIN I ain't sure what you want after you stood in silence for the last ten minutes.

FELIX I didn't hear the priest talkin' neither.

BENJAMIN This ain't his fight.

FELIX I spoke when I needed to.

BENJAMIN Don't get me wrong, it was a deserved respite from the noise normally comin' from you.

FELIX I listened, I watched her for deceit.

BENJAMIN And what did you see, Sheriff?

FELIX I ain't sure. But I reckon I trust her. She wants our land, we want to live, ain't no need for no more killin'.

BENJAMIN I feel there's somethin' brewin' I can't put my finger on.

FELIX She's keepin' her cards close, is all. I reckon it's a good deal and we should take it.

BENJAMIN I worked for years to clear the debts on that farm. My boys was born in that house, raised there. I ain't about to throw that away coz it's easier.

FELIX Easier than what? Gettin' killed?

BENJAMIN I've been fightin' the APR rather'n takin' the easy option. If I give in now, what's the point in all that? What've I been fightin' for?

FELIX I ain't sayin' it's easy to give in –

BENJAMIN I built that house myself. Learnt to cut timber, to frame, to seal out the wind and rain. Every second I spent buildin' I pictured grownin' old, dyin' and my boys takin' it from me. Everythin' I've done's been for them three boys. They're my legacy – when I die they're the only thing left of me on this world.

FELIX And if you die today? What happens then?

BENJAMIN Then I die fightin' for what's ours, for what's right.

FELIX You die and the APR will just ride in and take it from your children. You think they won't? You think there's anythin' stoppin' them from takin' it even after you're dead?

BENJAMIN Then they'll take it by force. I won't have given in; I won't have put my name on that document and signed away my children's birthright like a coward.

FELIX What of their right to a father? Huh? Jesus, Ben. You're gonna leave Caroline a widow. Leave them boys without a daddy. For what? Pride?

Silence.

You take this deal and you can go start a new life – build two houses if you want. Give Caroline a little girl. Take care of them boys and watch 'em become men. No one will think any less of you.

BENJAMIN What about your old lady, Felix? What about that house the two of you built?

FELIX She ain't comin' back, Ben. There's nothin' left of her in that house no more. Ain't no point me keepin' it like some damn tomb.

BENJAMIN I never thought you'd give in so easy.

FELIX It ain't been easy, Ben. We been fightin' for months. I have my cattle rode out, slaughtered. I had men try and kill me. And if we weren't trapped in here then maybe I'd think different. But I don't see no other way out. And I ain't keen to die.

BENJAMIN I don't know.

FELIX A house can be rebuilt. Think of your boys. Think of Caroline.

BENJAMIN They're all I'm thinkin' of.

FELIX I'm gonna sign, Ben. When she walks in here I'm just gonna sign. I can't fight no more. But my signature ain't worth a damn without yours. They need both our land to make their road. Please, Ben.

BENJAMIN Never thought I'd see you beggin'.

FELIX We ain't seen eye to eye on a whole lot, but that's just politics – this is our lives. Let's not throw them away.

BENJAMIN Alright.

FELIX You'll sign?

BENJAMIN I guess.

FELIX Thank you, Ben. What time is it?

BENJAMIN *(checking)* Less than a minute. You think I'm doin' the right thing, father?

MANOAH You must do as your heart tells you.

FELIX And your heart's tellin' you to sign – to live, to go back and see your children.

Knocking at the door.

LILLIAN *(off)* The clock's struck noon, gentleman.

FELIX I'm gonna let her in. Let me do the talkin' this time.

> **FELIX** *unbars the door.* **LILLIAN** *enters.* **FELIX** *closes the doors behind her.*

LILLIAN What a crisp and cool day it has turned into. I trust you've come to an agreeable decision, Mr Walker?

FELIX We've come to a decision alright.

LILLIAN Yes, Sheriff?

FELIX We're gonna sign them papers o' yours.

LILLIAN Excellent.

FELIX One condition.

LILLIAN Yes?

FELIX We gotta have your guarantee for our safety once them documents is signed. I ain't a fool, Miss Lily, I know you got fellas out there who seen us kill four of their buddies. I want your personal guarantee there'll be no retribution for our shootin' them dudes.

LILLIAN You have my word.

FELIX We can trust it?

LILLIAN I'll put my hand on the good book if you like? Father?

FELIX That won't be necessary, Miss Lily. I trust you – I'm thinkin' of fifteen minutes from now when your pa arrives.

LILLIAN His instructions are clear in this telegram, there is to be a peaceful resolution where possible and the deal is done at my sole discretion.

FELIX That's good enough for me. Well let's get this over with.

LILLIAN Excellent.

FELIX You want me to sign first, Ben?

No response.

I'll sign first. Then you can sign yours, Ben.

FELIX *signs one of the contracts.*

There you go, Miss Lily.

LILLIAN Mr Walker?

Silence.

For the good of the west, Mr Walker.

BENJAMIN I'm sorry. Father Manoah's right.

FELIX What?

BENJAMIN I gotta do what's in my heart.

FELIX You said you was gonna sign...

BENJAMIN I can't.

LILLIAN Felix?

FELIX He said he was gonna sign.

LILLIAN Mr Walker, need I remind you that my father will arrive in less than a quarter hour?

BENJAMIN I'm aware, Miss Davenport. I'm aware of my choice, but I can't sign your document. I'm sorry.

FELIX You gonna hang me out to dry? I already gone signed mine – you gonna let them take my land and not yours?

BENJAMIN I am sorry, Felix. Like you said, they need both our signatures to make it work.

LILLIAN That isn't entirely true, Mr Walker.

FELIX What?

LILLIAN The APR's primary objective was to acquire enough plots to lay the track to the west. Our secondary was to secure enough surrounding land that we might benefit financially from the development of the region. We've already secured the three plots required for development; all that remained was one of the two suitable plots for the continuation of the tracks.

BENJAMIN What three plots?

LILLIAN The widows of your fallen neighbours were far more obliging than their husbands had been. The deals were easy enough to secure.

BENJAMIN I ain't fallin' for your tricks, the women are long gone from here.

LILLIAN Long gone? They rode for Eden's Croft earlier this mornin'. They were particularly forthcomin' with their properties in the face of their recently deceased husbands.

BENJAMIN If you laid a hand on them –

LILLIAN The women and children are unharmed, Mr Walker. We're not monsters. They have accepted their deals and their land is now property of the American Pacific. Which brings me back to my earlier point, there were only two plots suitable for our tracks to the west, yours Mr Walker, and Mr Jackon's here. As Felix has been so kind as to sign his over, that will conclude our business for the day.

FELIX No.

LILLIAN No?

FELIX That ain't what we agreed.

LILLIAN Careful, Felix…

BENJAMIN What's goin' on here?

FELIX This ain't what we agreed.

LILLIAN The deal is clear in the contract you have just signed, Mr Jackson.

FELIX You know damn well that ain't the deal I'm talkin' 'bout.

LILLIAN I had assumed you'd rather keep the details of that arrangement from our mutual friend Mr Walker.

FELIX That's before you tried and stab me in the back.

BENJAMIN What arrangement, Felix? What've you done?

LILLIAN That's between you and the sheriff. I'll see myself out.

FELIX Like hell you will.

BENJAMIN You stay here, Davenport, 'til this is resolved. What deal you make, Felix?

LILLIAN Mr Jackson was under the belief that if he helped convince you to sell your land to the APR then we'd leave him be.

FELIX Under the belief? That was the deal.

BENJAMIN You snake…

LILLIAN That was the deal until you started shooting at APR men, Mr Jackson.

FELIX It's Sheriff Jackson – and I only fired coz your men was shootin' at me.

LILLIAN If they was shooting at you, Mr Jackson, you'd be dead.

FELIX They killed the other landowners.

LILLIAN I regret that.

FELIX How was I supposed to know they weren't gonna kill me?

BENJAMIN I can't believe my ears. You son of a bitch, Felix.

FELIX You'd have done the same. I was protectin' what's mine.

BENJAMIN You're job is to protect all of us, this whole community. But you sold us down the river to save your own land. You gave them a crack through which they've driven the spear.

FELIX It was just a matter of time 'til the APR got its way. You're a smart man, Ben, surely you know that.

BENJAMIN tears the sheriff's badge from FELIX's chest.

BENJAMIN You don't deserve to wear that tin star. You're a disgrace.

He throws it to the floor.

FELIX You'd have done the same, Ben.

BENJAMIN All the men who died today, you rode by their side, you pretended to be one of them.

FELIX I am one of them.

BENJAMIN No. You're one of the APR men now.

FELIX My Mary died in that house. She was my first sweetheart. I can't let that house go, can't let it be pulled to the ground. What else I got? You got family, wife, children.

BENJAMIN I can't believe you stood here and tried to convince me to sell for their good. I known some snakes in my day, ain't none of them compare to the poisonous pit viper that you shown yourself to be.

FELIX You ain't gonna tell no one 'bout this, Ben?

BENJAMIN You ought be marched down Main Street and tied to a stake, branded like the traitor you are.

FELIX Ben, I didn't have no choice –

BENJAMIN I'm gonna make sure there ain't a bar in the whole Bear State that'll let you drink alongside the men. I'll make sure every honest man from here to Washington knows the vermin you are.

FELIX Ben, please…

BENJAMIN Looks like you ain't gonna die in this chapel, but when the day comes, you'll die a rat all the same.

LILLIAN Now you gentlemen are finished, I hope you'll excuse me as I return to meet my father from the train. He'll be arriving shortly and keen to receive the wonderful news.

BENJAMIN Don't look so pleased with yourself, Davenport.

LILLIAN Thanks to Felix, I got what I came for.

BENJAMIN We're judged by our actions. One day, you'll be judged for yours. From what I seen today, you'll be lucky if you ain't swinging from a rope.

LILLIAN That your theory, Mr Walker? I done what I do for the good of the west. My father's name will go down in history as the man who completed the first transcontinental railroad and civilised this barren land. The men who got in the way – who've been discarded by the side of the tracks – ain't no one gonna remember their names.

BENJAMIN You tell yourself that if it helps you sleep at night.

LILLIAN You got pride, you got a sense of honor and dignity. You think that makes you a better man? Perhaps. But d'you think that makes a difference to who or what you are? No way.

BENJAMIN Just coz you dress nice and talk fancy don't make you any less of a whore, Miss Lily.

She laughs.

LILLIAN Wicked sense of humour, Mr Walker. I'm sorry for disturbing your day, father. You have a beautiful chapel.

MANOAH You should visit more often, Lillian. I'm sure the Lord would be eager to hear your prayers.

LILLIAN *(brandishing the contract)* Seems he's already answered them, father. Thank you, Felix. You've been a great help. I am sorry things have worked out this way for you.

She goes to leave.

You take care now.

FELIX *draws his revolver and takes aim at* **LILLIAN**.

FELIX No.

LILLIAN Felix…

MANOAH Sheriff…

FELIX You ain't leavin' with them papers.

LILLIAN Felix, that was about the most foolish thing you could have done. You realise that?

BENJAMIN Felix, you said yourself, land ain't worth dyin' over.

LILLIAN I came in under a truce, Felix. Now you go and raise your weapon at me. I had your word.

FELIX And I had yours.

LILLIAN Our deal changed. It's business.

FELIX So's this. Hand over them papers.

LILLIAN They're signed, Felix. Your property belongs to the American Pacific Railroad. You want to give the APR your life as well?

FELIX I ain't afraid of you.

LILLIAN What about my father? You ain't afraid of what he'll do to the man who holds a gun to his daughter?

MANOAH This will not end well for you, Sheriff. Lower your weapon.

FELIX You tear up them papers or I'll put lead in your gut and you can watch me tear 'em up as you bleed to death.

LILLIAN You kill me and not one of you is gonna get out of here alive.

BENJAMIN Felix, please. Think about this.

FELIX I let you go with them papers and I've lost everythin' anyhow. I might as well let your men kill me.

LILLIAN You'll be lucky if they just kill you. You shoot me and my father will make sure the last hours of your life are spent in such pain you'll be begging for a bullet in your skull.

FELIX You ever had a gun pointed at you before, Miss Lily?

LILLIAN I've not.

FELIX You don't seem mighty afraid?

LILLIAN Should I be?

FELIX *(screams)* You tear up them papers now!

BENJAMIN Felix!

> **LILLIAN** *holds her ground defiantly as* **FELIX** *makes his way towards her.*

LILLIAN You dare harm me…

FELIX Give me them papers.

LILLIAN It's not going to happen, Felix.

> **FELIX** *grabs her and pulls her in close. He presses the revolver into her flesh and pries the papers from her hand.*

Get your hands off me.

MANOAH Sheriff Jackson, this is a house of God. You will not harm her.

> **FELIX** *throws the papers to* **BENJAMIN**.

FELIX Tear them up, Ben.

BENJAMIN You're just makin' things worse for yourself.

FELIX Tear them up or I'm gonna put a bullet in her.

LILLIAN Don't do it, Mr Walker.

BENJAMIN You're makin' things worse for all of us, Felix.

FELIX Rip 'em up!

> *Resigned, very slowly* **BENJAMIN** *destroys the contract.*

LILLIAN You're making a very big mistake, Felix.

FELIX You shut your mouth. I heard enough from you.

BENJAMIN It's done, Felix. You let her go now.

FELIX It ain't done, Ben. This bitch deserves to pay.

MANOAH Sheriff…

BENJAMIN Felix, let her go.

LILLIAN You lay one finger on me –

FELIX Shut your god damn mouth! You're just a lyin' whore. You know what happens to lyin', cheatin' whores?

BENJAMIN Felix…

FELIX It's just like what you was sayin', Ben? People gonna be judged for their actions.

BENJAMIN Stop this…

FELIX Well you been judged Miss Lily and you been found guilty as hell. Time for your punishment.

> **FELIX** *drags* **LILLIAN** *towards the back room.*

MANOAH Benjamin, you must stop this.

> **BENJAMIN** *draws his revolver and takes aim at* **FELIX**. **FELIX** *holds* **LILLIAN** *between them.*

BENJAMIN I ain't gonna let you do this, Felix.

FELIX You proved you're a good shot and all, Ben, but there ain't no way you can shoot me without killin' Miss Lily. We both know that.

BENJAMIN You ain't this man.

FELIX You don't know what goddamn man I am!

BENJAMIN I know you ain't this.

FELIX She's treacherous, Ben. She's taken everythin' from me. She's gotta pay.

BENJAMIN Not like this. This ain't justice.

FELIX I'm the law man, ain't I? I'm the one who delivers justice.

MANOAH Felix…

FELIX Time to go, Miss Lily. Anythin' you want to say to the fellas 'fore we leave?

Silence.

No? Quiet as a mouse we've become. Well I'll get you moanin' soon enough.

FELIX drags her into the back room and shuts the door. We hear it lock from the inside.

BENJAMIN Jesus Christ…

MANOAH I can't see a way out of this, Benjamin.

BENJAMIN I don't reckon there is one.

MANOAH Perhaps not.

BENJAMIN Train's gonna arrive any minute.

MANOAH You should walk out there now and explain Felix's actions are not your own.

BENJAMIN You heard the lady, her rifleman won't give me that chance.

MANOAH When her father arrives, perhaps he will.

BENJAMIN When he comes in here to find his little girl's been raped and killed, you reckon he's gonna be in a talkin' mood?

MANOAH I'm trying to find some hope, Benjamin.

BENJAMIN I know. I'm sorry, father. I don't understand how everythin's turned out like this.

MANOAH Bad things happen to good men, Benjamin. And good things to bad.

BENJAMIN Maybe if I'd just signed…

MANOAH You followed your heart.

BENJAMIN And signed us all a death sentence.

MANOAH You weren't to know of Felix's deal. You couldn't predict his actions.

BENJAMIN I still can't believe he'd make a deal behind all our backs. Sell us down the river so he can sit out on his porch and watch us drown.

MANOAH You'd do anything to keep your home, Benjamin.

BENJAMIN Anythin'. But not that. You betray your neighbours – your friends – you ain't got no home to go to.

> **BENJAMIN** *rifles through the contract and papers dropped by* **LILLIAN**. *He picks up the telegram and reads it.*

I'll be damned…

MANOAH What is it?

BENJAMIN Lies.

MANOAH More lies?

BENJAMIN Seems everyone's full o' them, father.

MANOAH What does it contain?

BENJAMIN Somethin' that makes everythin' a whole lot more confusin'.

> *A gunshot rings out from the back room.*

Jesus Christ!

MANOAH Her men will have heard that.

BENJAMIN You best get yourself hidden away, father.

MANOAH I'll not say it again; I won't hide in my church.

BENJAMIN I ain't askin' you to hide – just keep your head down. I have guilt enough bringin' these men here without you gettin' hurt too.

BENJAMIN *looks through the shutter.*

They're comin'. They're movin' slow. But they're comin'.

MANOAH I'll say a prayer for you, son.

BENJAMIN Say a prayer for all of us, father.

A noise from the back room.

They're comin', Felix. You gone and done it now.

The door to the back room swings open. With the gun aimed at BENJAMIN, LILLIAN *enters. She looks battered and distressed, a spray of blood across her face.*

Jesus. Are you hurt?

LILLIAN No so bad as your friend in there.

BENJAMIN He ain't my friend.

LILLIAN He ain't nobody's friend now.

MANOAH Is he dead?

LILLIAN Unless a man can wake with a bullet through his temple.

MANOAH I see.

LILLIAN Son of a bitch deserved to die slow for what he was. Would that I had the time.

BENJAMIN Ain't no one here gonna dispute that. Your men heard the shot though. They're comin'.

LILLIAN You sound afeared, Mr Walker?

BENJAMIN For the padre. For the chapel.

LILLIAN I'm gonna show my face outside and buy us a few extra minutes. When I come back in, we're gonna finish this deal. And I'm done with talking polite.

BENJAMIN Understood.

> **LILLIAN** *crosses the room, keeping* **BENJAMIN** *in her sights. She steps outside.*

MANOAH The gun…

BENJAMIN I know…

MANOAH What are you going to do?

BENJAMIN I ain't sure.

> **LILLIAN** *re-enters, gun still held up.*

LILLIAN They seen I'm alive and seems the train's delayed. So we got time, but we better do this quick.

BENJAMIN What do you propose?

LILLIAN I'm going to talk with you honestly, Mr Walker.

BENJAMIN It's about time.

LILLIAN I won't tolerate your talking like that no more. Don't mistake me, Mr Walker; nothing is as it was before. You test me and I won't hesitate to put a bullet in you.

BENJAMIN Very well.

LILLIAN You got two choices. One. You sign that document so as when the train arrives I can return it to my father. Two. You refuse, my father arrives, he has his men come in here and use their knives on our dear padre. They'll cut him in a million ways you ain't never imagined and they won't stop 'til you put ink on that document. If that don't work, we'll bring your darling Caroline out here and pa's men will set themselves on her 'til you're begging to sign. If that don't work, you always got them sweet little boys –

BENJAMIN Alright! That's enough.

LILLIAN You gonna sign, Mr Walker?

BENJAMIN What's stoppin' me shootin' you right here and now?

LILLIAN You as blind as the padre? I have a gun pointed at you, Mr Walker.

BENJAMIN You want us to be honest with one another?

LILLIAN I do.

BENJAMIN That gun you're holdin' – it ain't loaded.

LILLIAN Bullshit. I just shot your buddy in the head with it.

BENJAMIN Using the last bullet. I'm sorry, Miss Lily, but your gun ain't loaded. This one, however…

BENJAMIN draws his revolver and takes aim.

This one's got a full chamber.

LILLIAN examines FELIX's gun. It is empty. She lowers it.

LILLIAN Why d'you let me talk so long, thinking I was armed?

BENJAMIN I wanted to see the woman you truly was.

LILLIAN And?

BENJAMIN There ain't an honest bone in your body, Miss Davenport.

LILLIAN That so?

The steam whistle pierces through the air. The train is approaching.

Time's running out, Mr Walker.

BENJAMIN How come?

LILLIAN Have you not been listening? My daddy's on that train and he's gonna resolve this one way or another.

BENJAMIN I've been honest with you 'bout that gun bein' empty. When you gonna start bein' honest with me?

LILLIAN I'm being honest, Mr Walker. I've warned you of the man that's coming here. I've told you truthful of what he's like to do. If I don't hand him that signed contract in the next two minutes he's gonna unleash hell.

BENJAMIN It's all lies, Miss Lily.

LILLIAN Lies?

BENJAMIN I read the telegram.

Silence.

You ain't got nothin' to say?

Silence.

Those men out there know the truth?

LILLIAN No one knows, except me and the doctors.

BENJAMIN There ain't no one on that train, father. Accordin' to this telegram, old man Davenport's been dead near three weeks. Why you been spinnin' this web, Lily?

LILLIAN My father may be dead, but his dream lives on.

BENJAMIN His dream?

LILLIAN The American Pacific Railroad – the great transcontinental railroad that will transform our world forever.

BENJAMIN You plan to finish it.

LILLIAN The APR's financers are expecting my father in D.C. in four months. When he doesn't show up they'll get suspicious.

BENJAMIN Suspicious financers? Don't sound good for business.

LILLIAN They learn he's dead and they'll pull all the funding. I know this railroad better than any man alive, but there ain't no way they'll let a woman in charge. A woman don't know her own mind. A woman's decisions is too clouded with emotion. A woman's temperament is too fragile for the complexities of business. Ain't that what you men think?

BENJAMIN Not all of us.

LILLIAN They'll find someone else to complete the road. After everything my daddy fought for, it'll be someone else's name goes down in history.

BENJAMIN So you're gonna finish it 'fore they find out.

LILLIAN So long as there are no delays, we'll have the railroad built within the four months. Time they find out my daddy's dead, our track will reach the ocean and it will be Davenport that saw it there.

BENJAMIN Not if you have to detour round every farm and homestead 'tween here and the Pacific.

LILLIAN It's business.

BENJAMIN Seems to me more than business.

LILLIAN You're right. It's about his legacy. It's about how he'll be remembered in history.

BENJAMIN Everythin' you've done, all the killin', the hurtin', it's been done by you, in your daddy's name.

LILLIAN I haven't done anything he wouldn't have, Mr Walker. My father would have done anything to complete this road.

BENJAMIN So where do we go from here?

LILLIAN I guess we better make a deal. The fact is, that truth doesn't change much for you, Mr Walker. You're still surrounded. You kill me, they come in here. You don't sign, I bring them in.

BENJAMIN 'Cept now I know somethin' you don't want them to know.

LILLIAN We'll make a businessman of you yet, Mr Walker. What do you want in exchange for this information remaining between the two of us?

BENJAMIN I'm gonna let you walk out there and you're gonna send a telegram to whatever dogs you got watchin' my family. My wife and boys are to be released immediately. I'll have your word – for whatever that's worth – that Father Manoah is to be unharmed. Once my family are in the clear, you signal back to me and I'll come out – unarmed.

LILLIAN How will I know you're not carrying?

BENJAMIN You'll take the guns with you when you leave.

LILLIAN And then what?

BENJAMIN I'll sign your document in front of all your men. I'll not say a word of your father's death. You'll hand me the money and we'll part ways.

LILLIAN As simple as that?

BENJAMIN Don't seem to me there's nothin' simple about it.

LILLIAN Why all this fighting if you're just gonna hand it over?

BENJAMIN I know when a battle's lost, Miss Davenport.

LILLIAN I respect that.

BENJAMIN Then we're agreed.

LILLIAN One more condition.

BENJAMIN What?

LILLIAN What occurred in that room, between your sheriff and me.

BENJAMIN Yeah.

LILLIAN You'll never mention it to another living soul. You'll not even whisper it alone in the desert. Is that clear?

BENJAMIN Worried about your reputation?

LILLIAN Is that clear?

BENJAMIN Crystal.

LILLIAN Good. Thank you. Your weapons.

> **BENJAMIN** *hands her his revolver and the repeater.*

That's all of them?

BENJAMIN Unless the priest has got one hidden in his cassock.

LILLIAN Very well. I hope we can trust each other now, Mr Walker?

BENJAMIN Almost everythin' you've said has been a lie.

LILLIAN It's nothing personal. I've been lying to the whole world for the last three weeks. But we must trust each other now – there are no more secrets. We both uphold our ends of the bargain and all will be well.

BENJAMIN Agreed.

LILLIAN I'm sorry to have caused you such a nuisance, father.

MANOAH I'm sorry for your suffering, child.

LILLIAN Everything heals in time.

MANOAH Farewell, Lillian.

LILLIAN I shall signal once the telegram has been received.

BENJAMIN Signal once my family have been released.

LILLIAN Of course.

> **LILLIAN** *exits the chapel with the contracts, the telegram and the three guns.*

> *The two men wait in silence.* **BENJAMIN** *watches through the shutter until* **LILLIAN** *is out of ear shot. He turns to* **MANOAH**.

MANOAH Do you trust her?

BENJAMIN No chance. You?

MANOAH I'm afraid not.

BENJAMIN That's somethin' comin' from a priest.

MANOAH What do you believe her intentions to be?

BENJAMIN She probably won't have my family released. She'll have me sign, then she'll have me killed. Then I reckon she'll come down here and seal any loose ends. She's got too much to lose letting the both of us live. If either story gets out then she's finished, the American Pacific is finished and her daddy's name's gone from history. That's too much risk for a woman like Lily Davenport.

MANOAH So what are you going to do?

BENJAMIN I can do what's easy, or I can do what's right.

MANOAH You are a good man, Benjamin Walker.

BENJAMIN No, I'm too proud – too stubborn. I should have signed the deeds over when I had the chance.

MANOAH You stood your ground.

BENJAMIN And now I'll never see my boys again – never hold Caroline again.

MANOAH Perhaps not in this life.

> *Silence.*

Wait here a moment. I have something for you.

BENJAMIN It ain't a secret tunnel out of here, by any chance?

MANOAH If only…

> **MANOAH** *goes into the back room.* **BENJAMIN** *looks through the shutter.* **MANOAH** *returns carrying a small wooden box.*

It's not been fired in many years.

He pulls a pistol from the box.

But I've kept it maintained and in good working condition.

BENJAMIN You are just full of surprises.

MANOAH I always knew it would come in use one day. I fear that day is now.

> **BENJAMIN** *takes the gun and checks it over.*

BENJAMIN There's one more thing I'd like to ask of you, father.

MANOAH Of course.

BENJAMIN I want you to hide. I'm sorry to ask it, but I need you to hide. There's only one person out there knows you're in here – and she'll be dead 'fore long. When the men come in they'll find Felix, but they mustn't find you.

MANOAH I see.

BENJAMIN You wait 'til they're gone. You mustn't make a sound. When all is over, I need you to try and find my family.

> **BENJAMIN** *hands* **MANOAH LILY** *'s pocket watch.*

If they're still alive, I'd like you to give them this. Tell Caroline of its value. Tell her to use it to get her and the boys safe.

MANOAH Of course.

BENJAMIN And tell her… Tell her I love her. I love her and I'm sorry.

MANOAH And the boys?

BENJAMIN Tell them to take good care of their ma. Tell them I'm proud of them all – been proud o' them every day since they was born. Tell them I love 'em.

MANOAH I will.

BENJAMIN Thank you, father.

> **BENJAMIN** *looks out of the shutter.*

There's the white flag.

> *He hides the gun under his jacket.*

MANOAH You'll be in my prayers, Benjamin.

BENJAMIN Better start prayin' now, father.

> **BENJAMIN** *opens the door and steps out, pulling the door closed behind him.*

> **MANOAH** *stands alone in the chapel. He turns to the altar and prays silently.*

> **MANOAH** *turns and looks towards the west before retreating into the back room.*

> *A single gunshot fills the air. It is followed in quick succession by many others.*

The End

The Frontier Trilogy: Volume III

The Rattlesnake's Kiss

CHARACTERS

1866

FATHER MANOAH – The priest at The Chapel of Emmanuel. 30-40. A noble and religious man, to be respected and feared.

US MARSHAL – A lawman from Texas. 25-30. A young gunslinger, theatrical in his demeanour, steady and confident.

1851

ELENA – Leon's former concubine, Mason's wife. 20-25. She is brave, fearless and kind-hearted.

SILAS – A Veneno Gang member. 25-40. He is cruel, poorly educated, and disturbing to watch.

JACK MASON – Former right hand man in the Veneno Gang. 20-25. He is the epitome of the dangerous yet remorseful gunslinger.

THEODORE LEON – Head of the Veneno Gang. 40-50. He is violent and bloodthirsty, but constantly level-headed. He is theatrical, deceitful and takes great pleasure in other's pain.

SETTING

The Chapel of Emmanuel, North of Canyon Falls, America
Summer 1866
&
Granja de Cerdos and La Meurte Negro, Northern Mexico
Summer 1851

NOTE ON DOUBLING

THEODORE LEON and SILAS can be performed by the same actor.
FATHER MANOAH and JACK MASON must be performed
by the same actor.

ACT ONE – 1866

Scene One – Santo Emmanuel

A hot summer's morning in the Chapel of Emmanuel where **FATHER MANOAH** *is preparing for a service. A black cloth covers his eyes – he is blind. A fierce wind blows across the desert outside.*

Through the doors steps a young man, he is dressed in a smart black suit and the star on his chest indicates he's a law official – **US MARSHAL**.

The **MARSHAL** *steps in and surveys the chapel in silence. Under one arm he carries a small wooden crate. He observes* **MANOAH** *who is aware of his presence, but neither man speaks.*

The silence is broken only by the wind outside.

After some time.

MARSHAL Ain't you gonna say nothin'.

MANOAH I assumed if you wanted to speak you would have done so already.

Silence.

MARSHAL The wind's hot. Comin' right off the dirt.

MANOAH It's often that way in summer.

Silence.

137

MARSHAL What's your name, padre?

MANOAH Father Manoah.

MARSHAL You baptised 'Father' or you got a Christian name?

Pause.

MANOAH Peter.

Silence.

MARSHAL Ain't you wonderin' who I am?

MANOAH You're here for the service? You're early – it doesn't start 'til ten.

MARSHAL I'm here to speak with you.

MANOAH Yes?

MARSHAL I need your assistance.

MANOAH How may I assist you?

MARSHAL I'm lookin' for a man. Member of your church.

MANOAH What do you want with him?

MARSHAL I'm here to arrest him.

MANOAH You're a lawman?

MARSHAL I'm a United States Marshal.

MANOAH This man must have done something serious. Who is he?

MARSHAL He's a killer.

MANOAH There are no murderers among this community.

MARSHAL There is one – I'm sure of it. My guess is he ain't killed no one for many years. But he's a killer all the same.

MANOAH What's his name?

MARSHAL I know the name he went by some years back. I been told I'll find him here at your service this mornin'. When the man arrives, I'm gonna need you to identify him to me.

MANOAH You don't know what he looks like?

MARSHAL Last time anyone saw him was fifteen years ago. I was only a boy at the time. So I'm gonna need you to point him out.

MANOAH Will you show me your badge?

MARSHAL You don't trust me?

MANOAH I need to know you are what you say you are before I hand over a member of my congregation.

MARSHAL Seems fair.

The **MARSHAL** *unpins his badge from his jacket and puts it in* **MANOAH***'s hand.*

Satisfied?

MANOAH *returns the badge.*

MANOAH You must tell me this man's name.

MARSHAL Fifteen years ago he went by the name of Jack Mason.

MANOAH What was the nature of his crime?

MARSHAL You know a fella named Jack Mason?

MANOAH There's a John Mason who lives in Davenport. Works as a tailor.

MARSHAL A tailor?

MANOAH Across the hills.

MARSHAL He comes here for service?

MANOAH He does. What d'you want him for?

MARSHAL Murder.

MANOAH As you said – what murder?

Silence.

MARSHAL You ever heard of the Veneno Gang, padre?

MANOAH Should I?

MARSHAL They were an outfit down on the border some years back. More than your average banditos – they was organised, sophisticated, led by a man named Theodore Leon.

MANOAH You say the name as if I should know it.

MARSHAL Leon had himself a fearsome reputation. Known in every border town 'cross Alta California. The Veneno Gang robbed payrolls, robbed banks, they robbed anythin' worth a damn and they used the money to fuel a lucrative and legitimate business in coal and ore mining in Northern Mexico.

MANOAH How is your Jack Mason connected to this?

MARSHAL He was Leon's right hand man. He was Leon's hired gun.

MANOAH I see.

MARSHAL Jack Mason was implicated in near a hundred murders connected to the Veneno Gang – not least the murder of the gang themselves.

MANOAH I don't follow…

MARSHAL Mason's final crime before his disappearance was the killin' of the entire Veneno Gang down at La Muerte Negro.

MANOAH He killed them all?

MARSHAL In one night. Jack Mason is a vicious and ruthless murderer.

MANOAH But the Veneno Gang were criminals themselves?

MARSHAL They were. And if he'd just killed Leon and his thugs then I guess I wouldn't be here today lookin' for him. As you say, they was criminals. But their women and children wasn't.

MANOAH I know Mason – he's not that man.

MARSHAL Trust me, Jack Mason is not what he may appear to be.

MANOAH How can you be sure it was Mason who killed them?

MARSHAL We got a witness.

MANOAH What witness?

MARSHAL A member of the Leon family. Kid went out to play by the creek, left camp with Mason there and his family alive, came back and they was all dead, 'cept Mason who was nowhere to be found.

MANOAH I see.

MARSHAL That was one of the first things I learned when investigatin' a crime – look for the man who ain't there no more.

MANOAH Absence does not always indicate guilt.

MARSHAL Ninety-nine times in a hundred, it does.

Silence.

So are you gonna point this fella out when he arrives?

MANOAH I will.

MARSHAL Well I'm most grateful to you. I've been huntin' this dude for some years now – today's a momentous occasion for me.

MANOAH I ask one thing…

MARSHAL Yeah?

MANOAH Will you wait until the service is over before you approach him? I should like for him to say his final prayers.

MARSHAL Final prayers? I ain't lookin' to hang the fella right here.

MANOAH If John Mason really is the man you say he is do you think he'll go peacefully and without a fight?

The **MARSHAL** *lets out a slow laugh.*

If he's to face you in a gun battle, at least let him make his peace with the Lord.

MARSHAL Very well.

MANOAH We have some time before he'll arrive.

MARSHAL You mind if I wait in here?

MANOAH Of course not.

MARSHAL It's a fine chapel. Santo Emmanuel – who was he?

MANOAH A martyr.

MARSHAL Yeah?

MANOAH He and forty two Christians were arrested and slaughtered for their belief.

MARSHAL Hardly worth dyin' for.

MANOAH What is?

MARSHAL A woman, gold, land…

MANOAH *laughs.*

Somethin' funny?

MANOAH What if you die in the line of duty, marshal? What will you have died for?

MARSHAL Justice.

MANOAH Is that so different from Saint Emmanuel? He believed in God, you in the law – you'd both be willing to die for those beliefs.

MARSHAL The law is real. Justice is real. One man takes a life; his life will be taken from him.

MANOAH That's your belief.

MARSHAL What's yours, padre? Forgiveness?

Silence.

Tell me, how can you forgive a man who don't ask for it? How do you forgive a man who won't repent?

MANOAH With great strength.

MARSHAL You think Jack Mason deserves forgiveness for his crimes?

MANOAH A long time has passed. Perhaps he's not the same man who committed those crimes?

MARSHAL Folk don't change all that much. Deep down we are what we are.

MANOAH Mason must have been a young man when he took those lives?

MARSHAL He was nineteen.

MANOAH He was a boy.

MARSHAL Your point?

MANOAH How old are you?

MARSHAL Twenty six.

MANOAH When you look back to the boy you were at nineteen, do you stand by his thoughts, his beliefs?

Silence.

There was a boy once, looked like me, shared my name, but he's not the man I am now.

MARSHAL In my business we judge folk by their actions, padre, not their beliefs. Jack Mason might think different, believe different than he did fifteen years ago, but that don't take away his actions – don't erase his crimes. If a crime is committed, justice must be brought upon the perpetrator.

MANOAH I can see we are at odds with one another.

MARSHAL We both believe a man is to be judged – you are prepared for him to be judged 'fore God. Me? I just want that judgement a little sooner, is all.

MANOAH Judgement and punishment are not the same thing, marshal.

MARSHAL I'm not here to judge the man, nor to punish him. I'm here to bring justice – that's all.

MANOAH Justice and vengeance are not the same either.

Silence.

What's in the crate?

MARSHAL A gift for Jack Mason.

MANOAH From whom?

MARSHAL An old friend.

MANOAH You working for the Pony Express as well as the United States Marshals?

MARSHAL Just doin' someone a favour.

Silence.

You speak Spanish, padre?

MANOAH Some.

MARSHAL You guess how the Veneno Gang got their name?

MANOAH I don't know.

MARSHAL Veneno – it's Spanish.

MANOAH Yes?

MARSHAL Means venom.

MANOAH I see.

MARSHAL Weren't just coz it sounded ominous neither. Theodore Leon had himself a flair for the theatrical. Word is if you made an enemy of him, and I'm talkin' about really pissin' the dude off, he wouldn't cut you, wouldn't hang you, wouldn't shoot you, he'd use the venom of a snake. Ever been bit by a snake, padre?

MANOAH I've not.

MARSHAL I once saw a little girl playin' in the tall grass – damn stupid thing to do in the summer – and all of a sudden she goes screamin', headin' for her mama, blood tricklin' down her leg. 'Fore she makes it home she hits the dirt and she's writhin' in agony. You know what you're meant to do when you see a snake?

MANOAH Stand still.

MARSHAL Exactly – you stand still, you count to thirty. I always says if you don't know how to count to thirty, just count to ten three times. Time you're done, that snake's forgot all about you and he's on his way. You panic, you try and strike out at that snake and sure as hell you're gonna get bit. Once the venom's in you, if you can't suck it out, you just got to play calm – you best to sit down in the shade and wait for someone to come along. That little girl, she goes runnin', screamin' for her mama, every breath she draws in, every step forward, her little heart's pumping blood and venom faster and faster round her body.

MANOAH That's dreadful.

MARSHAL Sure was. Took her some hours to die. Whole town could hear the screams – the fever took hold and all she dreamed was that snake lungin' for her again and again. Weren't venom that killed that little girl – it was fear. It was fear made her run from the snake, fear that kept her screamin' through the night, fear that stopped her heart in her chest. That's what Theodore Leon knew, fear. He knew the fear instilled in men's minds at the sight of his gang, even at the name – Veneno.

MANOAH I can imagine.

Silence.

MARSHAL What happened to your eyes?

MANOAH I lost my sight.

MARSHAL How?

MANOAH I stared too long into the sun.

MARSHAL Didn't you know that was bad for you?

MANOAH I do now.

MARSHAL How come you keep 'em covered?

MANOAH For the sake of others.

MARSHAL For the comfort of others? That's generous of you.

Silence.

What d'you do before you was a priest?

MANOAH What everyone else does, I farmed.

MARSHAL Farmed what?

MANOAH Pigs.

Silence.

MARSHAL Well don't let me keep you, padre, if you got work to be doin'.

MANOAH Thank you.

MANOAH *continues to prepare for the service. The* **MARSHAL** *begins to sing to himself.*

MARSHAL

IN THE COLD AND DARK OF WINTER
I JOURNEYED FAR TO SEE MY LOVE.
EVERY DROP OF SNOW WOULD LINGER,
A PAINFUL JEST FROM HIM ABOVE.

My singin' ain't a nuisance to you is it?

MANOAH Not at all.

MARSHAL You know the tune?

MANOAH I do not.

MARSHAL It ain't a church song.

He continues to sing, more loudly this time.

THE WHITE LAELIA GREW ABOUT HER,
IT STOOD SO PROUD, ALONE AND BRAVE,
UPON THE TREES AMONG THE FOREST,
UPON THE TREES ABOVE HER GRAVE.

Another voice joins the song. It is **ELENA***'s.* **MANOAH** *does not hear it.*

BOTH

IN THE GROUND BELOW THE MOUNTAINS,
SHE HAD LAIN FOR THIRTEEN YEARS,
BUT COME THE WINTER I WOULD JOURNEY
TO WARM HER TOMB WITH FALLING TEARS.
THE WHITE LAELIA GREW ABOUT HER,
IT STOOD SO PROUD, ALONE AND BRAVE,
UPON THE TREES AMONG THE FOREST,
UPON THE TREES ABOVE HER GRAVE.

ACT TWO – 1851

Scene One – Veneno

*It's late morning in the homestead of **MASON***'s *Granja de Cerdos. The summer wind blows outside.*

ELENA *sings to herself as she works, bringing a pail of water in from the well. She appears weary; her skin is dark with dust, her hands cracked and raw from labor.*

ELENA
> THE WHITE LAELIA GREW ABOUT HIM,
> IT STOOD SO PROUD, ALONE AND BRAVE,
> UPON THE TREES AMONG THE FOREST,
> UPON THE TREES ABOVE HIS GRAVE.

She stops singing abruptly as the door swings open and **SILAS** *enters.*

A long silence.

My husband will be back any moment.

SILAS How nice for you.

ELENA You take another step inside this house and I'll level you with this bucket.

SILAS Ain't no way to greet a guest now, is it?

ELENA What d'you want?

SILAS I took the place to be empty.

ELENA Well it ain't so get goin'.

SILAS I can see it ain't.

ELENA What you lookin' for, mister?

SILAS Someone a mite friendlier than you.

ELENA You ain't given me cause for friendliness.

SILAS I ain't given you no cause for anger neither.

ELENA You walkin' in my house is cause enough.

Silence.

SILAS I'm lookin' for the home of Jack Mason.

ELENA Ain't never heard of him.

SILAS I reckon you have.

ELENA I tell you I don't know the man.

SILAS I got it on good authority I'd find him on this here farm.

ELENA Ain't no one here but me and, in a few minutes, my husband.

SILAS And who is your husband?

ELENA Ain't none of your concern.

SILAS Fear it might be.

ELENA You best leave immediate 'fore he gets back.

SILAS I ain't leavin'.

ELENA You best.

SILAS I had it on good authority Jack Mason resides here. I gone told my boss that same information.

ELENA What boss?

SILAS The boss man. The man I work for.

ELENA Who is he?

SILAS Theodore Leon.

ELENA*'s face falls.*

So you know who he is.

ELENA I've heard of him.

SILAS I may not know you by sight, Elena, but Leon sure will, and you sure fit his description. Though I must say you ain't the rare flower I took you to be.

ELENA My husband will be back any moment. If he sees you here –

SILAS Come nightfall, Leon and the rest of the Venenos is gonna be here for Jack. Leon's sent me ahead to make a deal with you.

ELENA Jack will never make a deal.

SILAS I ain't lookin' to Jack, I'm looking to you, Elena.

ELENA Well I ain't lookin' for a deal neither.

SILAS You best hear it first. That way I can ride back to Leon and let him know at least I done my piece.

ELENA What does he want?

SILAS He wants Jack.

ELENA And?

SILAS He'll let you go. He'll give you money enough to start afresh. There'll be no repercussions.

ELENA In exchange for what?

SILAS In exchange for Jack.

ELENA What would he have me do?

SILAS, *grimacing, pulls a small corked medicine bottle from his coat and places it between the two of them.*

I ain't gonna do no harm to my husband.

SILAS Course not, that ain't what Leon's askin'. Just that you help us out a little.

Silence.

You know what's in that bottle?

ELENA Of course.

Silence.

SILAS You ever seen your husband shoot?

ELENA I've not.

SILAS Me neither. But I'm guessin', as I have, that you've heard the stories?

ELENA People talk.

SILAS Sure do. If Jack's half as good a shot as folk say he was... Well... That'd scare any man from goin' against him, wouldn't it?

ELENA I guess so.

SILAS I heard he once killed an entire posse down in San Sebastian usin' a single revolver and only six shots. That true?

ELENA I wouldn't know.

SILAS He not talk about it much? Not talk about the old days when he rode with Leon?

Silence.

You must miss them days – miss the old way of life? I reckon a whore learns to enjoy her work, easy as it is, lyin' on her back.

ELENA Any half decent whore would make you think they enjoyed it. Fact you're fooled says more about you than them.

SILAS *laughs.*

SILAS I heard he once killed a bear with nothing but his hands and a six inch blade. You heard that one?

ELENA I heard the one where he walked on the water and turned his own piss into whiskey.

SILAS You got a whore's mouth. You look the part of a little farm wife alright, but you're exactly as they said you would be.

ELENA What do they say about me?

SILAS That you were as sweet a place as any for a man to rest his cock.

ELENA I heard fellas say the same of you.

SILAS I can understand why you went with Jack – a young fella offerin' adventure. This what you expected when you signed up? Livin' on a shit-stinkin' farm in down in Mexico?

ELENA It weren't shit-stinkin' 'til you walked in.

SILAS You keep openin' your mouth to me like that and I'm gonna stick somethin' in it.

Silence.

What d'you reckon about this here bottle then? Reckon you can help old Leon out?

ELENA What choice do I have?

SILAS You help him out or he'll find another way to get Jack. If he has to find another way then you'll have pissed him off. You know what Leon's like when he's pissed off.

ELENA So I give him Jack, or we both die? Don't sound like Leon's changed one bit.

SILAS You know what they say – if it ain't broke.

ELENA Theodore Leon's been broke since the day he was born.

SILAS You want me to tell him that?

No response.

I didn't reckon so. You got an answer you want me to give him?

ELENA I need time to think.

SILAS You ain't got none.

ELENA I need time.

SILAS How about you give me a free one while you make up your mind?

ELENA There ain't no free ones and there ain't no paid ones neither.

SILAS Shame.

ELENA I ain't a workin' girl no more.

SILAS You don't want to be a workin' girl again then you best take this deal.

ELENA You best leave 'fore Jack comes back.

SILAS What's your answer for Leon?

ELENA Tell him to come for Jack. If Leon's alive by mornin', then he'll know I've helped him out.

SILAS And if he ain't alive?

ELENA Then Jack will have killed every last one of you.

SILAS You better make the right decision.

ELENA You get outta here.

SILAS Been a pleasure meetin' you, Miss Elena.

ELENA Get out.

SILAS Them's fine animals your fella's got out there. When all this is over perhaps you'll cook me up a decent cut of pork?

No response.

I'll be on my way.

SILAS *leaves.* **ELENA** *sits alone; she looks at the medicine bottle.*

Outside in the distance we hear gunshots. She runs to the door and outside.

Moments later she returns with **JACK MASON**. *He is wounded; a bullet has grazed his right arm.*

ELENA *helps him in and grabs a cloth to stem the bleeding.*

JACK Who was he?

ELENA You ain't gonna like it none.

JACK Tell me…

ELENA Leon sent him here.

JACK Oh, Jesus. How'd he find us?

ELENA Didn't say.

JACK What he want?

ELENA Wanted you.

JACK He didn't harm you?

ELENA No.

JACK Didn't touch you at all? If he laid a finger on you –

ELENA I'm fine. It's you I'm worried about.

JACK It's just a graze – it'll heal. Tell me what that man wanted.

ELENA Wanted me to help Leon capture you.

JACK What'd you say?

ELENA I said no, of course.

JACK And he just left?

ELENA Said he'd tell Leon and Leon would come back
with his men and find another way to get you. I ain't
never seen you wounded before – how'd he get the
draw on you?

JACK Caught me off guard. Was comin' over the brow of
the hill – the wind's up, had my head down.

ELENA It hurt?

JACK It's just through the flesh. He say where the boys
are?

ELENA No. I'm guessin' they ain't camped far.

JACK Ain't like Leon to send a scout.

ELENA He's afraid of you.

JACK He's right to be.

ELENA What are we gonna do?

JACK *We* ain't gonna do nothin'. I'm gonna finish this.

ELENA You can't go against them all.

JACK I been outnumbered before.

ELENA You don't know how outnumbered you are.

JACK If I don't finish this then we're gonna be lookin'
over our shoulder the rest of our days.

ELENA We can get out. We go further, right the way north.

JACK Don't matter how far we go, don't matter what
names we give ourselves – no one quits the Venenos.
You know that – no one. They will find us.

ELENA We go far enough, for long enough and he'll give
up.

JACK Give up? I stole from him, Elena.

ELENA What?

JACK I stole you.

ELENA I weren't his.

JACK You were his just as I was. You know Leon, he ain't interested in sharin', he either owns you or he kills you. Every man that fights by his side will fight until they die. Every woman who lays with him is no different. I left – I betrayed him.

ELENA Betrayed?

JACK In *his* eyes.

ELENA That night you came to the house you promised we'd go and all this would be behind us.

JACK I know.

ELENA You promised your days of killin' were behind.

JACK I meant it.

ELENA But you just killed a man not five minutes past.

JACK Of course I did. I had to.

ELENA And you'll kill more.

JACK I have to.

ELENA You don't. Let's just run and not look back.

Silence.

What if he kills you? Huh? What happens when you don't come back to me? What's to stop Leon ridin' right up here and puttin' a bullet between my eyes?

JACK I won't let him.

ELENA Can you hear yourself? You think you're invincible? You just got shot – you even able to lift your gun?

JACK I can lift my gun just fine. There ain't no point in us spittin' at each other this.

ELENA You're gonna die tonight.

JACK I got my strength. Ain't nothin' they can do to take that away. There's not one of them can rival me in a fight – you know that, Leon knows that. I'm not sayin' I'm invincible, I know I ain't, but with a loaded six shooter in my grip I'm as damn near as any man is like to come.

Silence.

ELENA Please…

JACK I'm sorry. I have to do this.

Silence.

Will you fetch some cloth to plug this hole?

ELENA Of course.

ELENA *collects more scraps of cloth to make a bandage.*

JACK Everythin's gonna be fine.

No response.

You trust me, Elena?

No response.

Elena?

ELENA I trust you. Here, let me put some ointment on it – make sure it don't fester.

JACK Thank you.

ELENA *reveals the bottle handed over by* **SILAS***. She carefully tips the contents into a scrap of cloth.*

Before I ride out I'll drop that dude's body in with the pigs. If anyone's comin' past it ain't gonna look good to have a corpse lyin' on our land.

ELENA They'll make quick work of him. Now you hold still – this is gonna sting somethin' fierce.

JACK Sometimes I reckon this medicine does more damage than good.

> **ELENA** *holds the cloth to his wound – he recoils in pain.*

Jesus!

ELENA Hold still – it's doin' its work.

JACK Burns like fire.

ELENA Quit whinin' like a child.

> **JACK** *laughs.*

JACK I'd like to see a child suffer this torture you're puttin' on me.

> *She wraps the wound in the makeshift bandage.*

ELENA That's just the healin'. There you go, all done.

JACK Ain't gonna be no more bullet holes after tonight, Elena. You got my word.

> *Silence.*

Will you fetch me out a smoke?

ELENA What for?

JACK For after.

ELENA That your tradition?

JACK Somethin' like that.

ELENA Seems you make an easy transition back to your old ways.

JACK It's just a cigarillo.

ELENA For you to smoke after you take a man's life.

JACK I know what you seen today must frighten you – I know this is the world we left behind. But leavin' somethin' behind don't mean you're rid of it. I made choices in my life I ain't proud of, but without them I'd never have made it here – here with you. I don't want to fight Leon, I don't want to kill him; I want to be with you and I want you to be safe. If I'm gonna keep you safe then for one more night I'm gonna be the killer I used to be. Just one more time, and then we'll be free from him. And I ain't talkin' 'bout Leon – I'm talkin' about the man I was when I met you. After tonight, we'll be rid of him and we won't never have to talk on him again.

Silence.

Alright?

ELENA Alright.

JACK You know I love you, Elena. Love you more than anythin'.

ELENA Yeah.

JACK Yeah?

ELENA Yeah, I know.

JACK And you love me?

ELENA Of course.

JACK Then I'll fight – one last time.

No response.

How 'bout you fetch out that smoke?

ELENA *collects a cigarillo and a pack of matches. She puts them in his jacket pocket.*

JACK *checks his revolver and reloads a shot.*

Wait, there's somethin' missing.

He leaves for a moment and returns carrying an old leather duster.

He pulls on the coat and positions his gun belt.

I look the part?

ELENA Every inch the gunslinger.

JACK Just for tonight. Once I'm done with Leon, we can burn this duster and hurl this peacemaker in the flames alongside it.

ELENA How will you find his camp?

JACK That dude's horse is still tied up. I'll set him lose and follow him. Reckon he'll lead me right back.

ELENA I'm sorry that it's come to this.

JACK Ain't your fault, Elena.

ELENA All the same, I'm sorry.

JACK Me too.

He kisses her.

I'll see you before the sun's up.

He turns to go but stops before he reaches the door. He raises his right hand slowly and takes it in his left.

My fingers... They're numb.

He touches the wound through his coat.

Jesus! Elena, somethin's wrong...

ELENA I'm sorry.

JACK My whole arm, it's swellin' up.

He slowly sinks to the floor, clutching his arm.

ELENA I'm so sorry, Jack...

JACK What've you done? Elena?

ELENA You know I loved you.

JACK What have you done?

He is becoming feverish. His eyes dart around the room as if he can see figures moving.

You've killed me, Elena...

Slowly, the room begins to fade away into darkness. The sound of his heart thumping heavily fills **JACK***'s ears.*

ELENA*'s voice floats gently over the noise.*

ELENA
WITH EACH STEP INTO THE DEEP,
I CLOSE MY EYES AND TEARS I WEEP,
FOR THE LIGHT WILL SOON BE DIM,
I'LL MOURN THE LIFE THAT COULD HAVE BEEN.

BENEATH THE EARTH, THE EYES ARE CHOKED,
WRAPPED IN DARKNESS, BOUND AND CLOAKED.
ALL THE STONE THAT HOLDS ME SAFE
IS SOON TO BE MY NARROW GRAVE.

Scene Two – La Muerte Negro

Pitch black darkness fills the mines as the hot summer's wind blows and whistles through the caverns and tunnels.

A deep, haunting voice comes through the darkness.

LEON

> IN THIS TOMB, MY SIX BY THREE,
> THE LORD SHAN'T COME TO RESCUE ME
> FOR I AM LOCKED AWAY FROM HIM
> AS PUNISHMENT FOR ALL MY SINS.

A cry of pain fills the air.

JACK *(rasping)* Who's there?

LEON

> FOR I AM LOCKED AWAY FROM HIM
> AS PUNISHMENT FOR ALL MY SINS.

JACK Who is that? Who's out there?

LEON Been so long you don't recognise my voice?

JACK Leon?

LEON That fever must have got to your brain.

JACK Leon, is that you?

LEON Just relax, kid.

JACK I can't see anythin'…

LEON No…

JACK It's so dark…

LEON Just relax…

JACK What's happened?

LEON You need to stay calm, kid. Get too excited and your heart's gonna pump that venom right through you.

JACK Please, tell me what's happened. My eyes…

LEON Your eyes ain't gonna work no more, Jack. I'm sorry to say.

JACK What've you done?

LEON It ain't what I done, kid, it's what you done. It's what you done to me that's come back 'round and done to yourself.

JACK Where are we?

LEON We're in a mine. It belongs to me, to the Venenos. We're right 'neath the hills in a labyrinth of coal-filled rock.

JACK Please tell me what's happened…

LEON What's happened is you gone and walked out on us. What's happened is you tried to turn your back on your family and leave us all behind. You betrayed your family, Jack. You thought you could just run from us, but I got eyes and ears right across this country and there ain't nowhere to hide for the legendary Jack Mason, the kid who butchers with one glance of the eye.

JACK I'm not that man any more.

LEON Clearly – you ain't got the eyes to glance with.

JACK What did you do?

LEON You stared too long at the sun, kid. That's what dreamin' is, it's staring into the bright light of the sun and hopin' for somethin' better. But there ain't nothin' better out there and all your starin' gets you is two burned out eyes and no chance in hell your life's gonna improve none from that.

JACK You took them?

LEON Remember the old man in San Sebastian? The priest who told the Governor where we was hidin' out? You recall what I did to him?

No response.

He used his tongue against me. So I tied him down, soaked the point of my knife in venom and I ran it across his tongue. Within the hour his tongue swelled to the size of an ox's. You recall what I said to you that day? You recall my reasonin'?

No response.

I wanted it so every time that old fella tried to speak for the rest of his miserable life he'd think of me, of the Venenos, and he'd sure as hell never use that tongue against one of us again. And every man who met him would know what happens when you use your tongue against Theodore Leon. So you understand, when I dragged your body to the centre of camp and pierced your eyes with that poisoned blade, it weren't to punish you, Jack, it were as a warnin' to all the other boys that they best not look for nothin' better, or they'll get their eyes burned too.

JACK *sobs almost inaudibly.*

I didn't want to do it. You don't leave the Venenos, kid, you knew that. When you sign up you put your life in my hands. You wanna leave? That's fine, but your life stays with me. We had things good, kid. Why would you go and ruin somethin' so perfect?

JACK We're nothin' perfect 'bout what we had. Was just killin' and stealin' and killin' some more.

LEON You never raised issue with it.

JACK Would you have listened if I had?

LEON We were a team, you and me. All of us was family.

JACK I'd taken so many lives, I'd had enough. It was my choice.

LEON A family like ours is built on respect – it works on a careful balance, kid, you know that. You can't take from us, you can't benefit from us without payin' somethin' back in. That's the balance we have that keeps this outfit runnin'. You lived a decent life with us, you was never short of money to burn, whiskey to drink, women to spoil. In exchange for those comforts I asked you to raise your gun and defend the men who helped provide them.

JACK You didn't never ask.

LEON I didn't have to. You wanted this lifestyle; you wanted to be a part of the Venenos.

JACK I was young, I didn't know any better.

LEON You can't blame your naivety on me, Jack.

JACK My whole life I wanted to be like you, 'til the day I realised what you really was.

LEON And what's that?

JACK You ain't a good man.

LEON And you are?

JACK No. But I wanted to be one.

LEON Where's that got you? I'll tell you where, at the bottom of a coal mine strapped to a barrel of gunpowder and a half dozen sticks of dynamite.

JACK What's wrong with a bullet?

LEON Don't flatter yourself – that dynamite ain't for you. I'm bringin' this whole place down come mornin'. You bein' inside? Well that's just a charmin' coincidence.

JACK Why wait 'til mornin'? Why not get it over with?

LEON You know what I'm afraid of, Jack?

JACK I didn't take you to be afeared of nothin'.

LEON Not many things. I'd face my death knowingly, I'll catch a snake with my hands and tease the venom from its kiss, but at the end of the day, when the sun goes to bed and the light goes out across the land, that scares me.

JACK You're afraid of the dark?

LEON The dark is the only thing a man should fear. When you can't see to protect your loved ones, ain't that somethin' to fear? When you can't see what's ahead nor what's behind, ain't that somethin' to fear? When a man can't see his own death comin', ain't that somethin' to fear? Darkness, it's the only time a man is truly alone. In the dark there ain't no one to watch over you, there ain't no God, it's just you and whatever beast wants to end your life. Don't that scare you?

Silence.

Real soon I'm gonna walk out to the camp and I'm gonna open myself a bottle. When that bottle's empty I'm gonna find myself a woman. When I'm done with that woman I'm gonna sleep. And when I wake, I'm gonna light the fuse that leads right down here to you. 'Tween now and then, you're gonna sit down here in the dark. The rats is gonna run over your skin and gnaw at your flesh. You're gonna feel more alone that you ever done before. By mornin', by the time that fuse is lit, trust me, you're gonna be afeared of the dark just as I am.

The flicker of a candle flame illuminates in the darkness.

From the gloom, **ELENA** *appears. As the light reaches*
JACK, *he looks up to see her.*

JACK Elena?

ELENA Jack...

JACK I'm sorry, Elena –

ELENA You need to stay calm, Jack. The fever...

JACK You was right, we should have got out. I should have
listened.

ELENA The venom's in your blood. It's causin' you a fever.
You're seein' things, is all.

JACK I just wanted to protect you, to keep you safe – to
take you away from him, from that life.

The light starts to fade.

Elena?

ELENA Elena's not here, kid.

The light fades more.

JACK Don't leave.

ELENA I told you, I'm gonna leave here 'til mornin', Jack.

Darkness has come again.

JACK Elena?!

LEON Why is it you want to see her, kid?

JACK What did you do to her?

LEON You're seein' things, kid. It's the fever – the venom –
you need to relax, don't fight it.

JACK Where is she?

LEON If I were you I wouldn't care so much about the girl.

JACK If you harmed her...

LEON Don't you remember the events that brought you here, Jack? Can't you remember what she done?

JACK What are you talkin' about?

LEON I thought you'd have remembered.

JACK Remembered what, dammit?

LEON I'm sorry to be the one to tell you this, kid, but it was Elena who gave you over to us.

JACK Never…

LEON Yeah.

JACK She'd never…

LEON Must be cruel to hear.

JACK I don't believe you.

LEON How else you think you ended up here?

JACK I –

LEON Silas, the fella I sent out to make the offer, he didn't never return to camp – as no doubt you are aware. But his horse did. That mare comes ridin' straight up the track to the mine. Jack Mason wants a fight, I guessed. That was 'til I seen our sweet Elena ridin' up the track behind that loose mare with a young man swung over the back of the horse. Like a sack o' potatoes you was. None of this ring any bells?

No response.

That cut on your arm – she fixed it with the venom of a pit viper. I'm sorry, kid, but she done stabbed you right in the back. Ain't that a sorry tale? I guess you can take the whore out the brothel…

Silence.

JACK What did you offer her?

LEON What every workin' girl wants – money.

JACK She didn't want no money.

LEON Everyone says that 'til you offer them enough. What choice did she have, kid? You expect her to slave on that pig farm the rest of her life?

JACK We were happy…

LEON Tellin' yourself that don't make it true. I know you better than anyone, kid, some men are made for slingin' pig shit, some ain't.

Silence.

You know what the locals call this place?

No response.

La Muerte Negro. It means 'the black death'. So many of their people have died down here. Cave ins, coal dust in the lungs, accidents with dynamite – take your pick. When I bought this place the fella didn't mention nothin' about it – kept his mouth shut. So now I got myself a coal mine that the locals are afraid of. Fear's a real useful tool to get men to do your biddin'. But that don't work so well when the thing they fear is the same thing you're tryin' to get 'em to do. I mean to make a fortune from this mine, that ain't gonna happen if I can't get no coal out.

JACK Why don't you get down on your hands and dig it yourself?

LEON Just as you ain't made for slingin' shit, so I'm not made for breakin' rock. No, I got myself a much better idea. You ever heard of insurance?

No response.

The banks use it to protect their gold. Means if some transients come through town and ride out with their money the bank gets paid by the insurers for the worth of that gold. I done the same thing with this mine. Tomorrow mornin' when the powder and dynamite you're strapped to blows, it's gonna ignite the sticks in the tunnel next to us, that'll ignite the sticks in the tunnel over, igniting more sticks in the next tunnel and so on. One match is gonna bring down this entire mountain, every last rock. Once it has, I'm gonna ride out to my insurance fella, and he's gonna pay me every damn peso this hole is worth. Now, ain't that better than diggin' in the dark with my own hands?

Silence.

You know your mother's here?

JACK What?

LEON Sure, up in the camp. Got the whole family. We're moving out in the mornin' right before this place goes up.

JACK Peter's here?

LEON Little Peter's one of us now, kid. He ain't quite the shot you was, but give him some time and he'll be shootin' just like his big brother.

JACK He's just a boy, you gotta let him go.

LEON He's family – don't you understand? My family takes care of each other, Jack.

JACK *laughs.*

JACK You hear yourself, Leon? Family? Can't you see the irony of that when you're down here with your own son strapped to a barrel of gunpowder?

LEON Weren't it you just tellin' me you ain't that man no more? Accordin' to you my son's already dead. He died the night he rode out of camp with that whore, Elena. Ain't that about right?

JACK I didn't want to be a part of this no more.

LEON You was born to be a part of this. You was meant for it. I gave you everythin' a father has to give, and you betrayed me.

JACK Will you make me one promise?

LEON What?

JACK When Peter's old enough, will you give him the choice? Will you ask him what he wants?

LEON Sure, if it'll ease your passin', then I'll ask him.

JACK And will you listen? Will you hear what he says?

LEON Sure I'll listen. And if he's got sights for somethin' better, I'll run venom on my blade and I'll take his eyes. Don't no one leave the Venenos, kid. Especially not my own boys.

Silence.

All this talk's given me a thirst. I'm gonna head up top and drink down some whiskey. I'll leave you to your thoughts.

JACK Please, Leon... Father...

LEON I remember why I never wanted you to call me that – makes me feel so old. Goodnight, kid. Sweet dreams.

LEON *leaves* **JACK** *in the darkness.*

A voice floats across the darkness. A flicker of candlelight appears and **ELENA** *is there.*

ELENA
FEVER SPIKED AS MY HEART RACED
TORE THROUGH MY BONES NOW I'M LAYIN' WASTE
WATCHING THE DUST AS IT SETTLES
THE SUN BEATS DOWN AGAIN

JACK Elena?

ELENA It's okay Jack.

JACK Elena, how could you? How could you betray me like this?

ELENA It weren't me betrayed you, Jack. I'm sorry, I never wanted no harm to come to you, I never wanted any of this.

JACK The venom?

ELENA I didn't have no choice, Jack. I asked you not to fight, I begged you for the two of us to leave and not look back.

JACK But I couldn't!

ELENA Of course you could, if you'd wanted to. But you didn't want to. And now I know why, because you're Jack Mason, and you always will be. No matter how much you say it ain't so and no matter how hard you fight to leave this life behind you it will always catch you in the end.

JACK I wanted to leave it behind. I truly did, I swear it.

ELENA I know you did, Jack, but this is the man you were born to be – there ain't no escapin' that.

JACK I wanted the two of us to have a new life together. I wanted a better life for you.

ELENA I know that, and I'm so grateful. Ain't no one ever been so kind to me before. I'm sorry for how things have turned out.

JACK No, don't apologise. This is my doing, I am entirely to blame, and it's me who must ask your forgiveness.

ELENA There's nothin' to forgive, Jack. The wolf doesn't ask forgiveness when it slaughters a deer. The snake doesn't ask forgiveness when it bites its prey. You are the man you are, Jack, don't ask forgiveness for that.

ELENA *begins to sing once more.*

SCORCHED AS THE EARTH AND I'M DYING
MY BREATH GIVES UP HOPE, GIVES UP TRYING
CLAWING THE WIND THAT KEEPS BLOWING
THE SUN BEATS DOWN AGAIN

She goes to **JACK** *and unties his bonds. She reveals a black cloth which she gently ties around his head, covering his eyes.*

I'LL NEVER
PLAY THE FOOL WITH A GUN
I'LL NEVER
RAISE MY EYES TO THE SUN
I'LL NEVER
I'LL NEVER

She kisses him tenderly before fading away into the darkness.

BLOODIED TEARS FALL AS ASHES,
THE DIRT ON MY LIPS NOW MY CASKET.
MOURNING MY LIFE AS IT POURS AWAY
AND THE SUN BEATS DOWN AGAIN.

ACT THREE – 1866

Scene One – La Serpiente De Cascabel

The **U.S. MARSHAL** *and* **FATHER MANOAH** *sit in silence.*

A ticking from the **MARSHAL**'s *pocket watch fills the silence, punctuating each second.*

After some time.

MARSHAL I gotta ask, padre. What you plannin' on doin' when the service starts?

MANOAH I don't follow your meaning.

MARSHAL I mean when the town folk arrive and you gotta point one of them out to me as Jack Mason. What are you gonna do?

MANOAH I hadn't worked that out yet.

There is a stillness. Suddenly, **MANOAH** *grabs a shotgun from under the altar and takes aim but he's too slow. The* **MARSHAL** *has ducked away from the spot where* **MANOAH** *is aiming and has his revolver out and pointed at the priest.*

He slowly cocks it. **MANOAH** *realises he's been beat. He lowers the shotgun.*

How long have you known?

MARSHAL Since I walked in.

MANOAH Why didn't you say anything?

MARSHAL I reckoned there weren't no harm in waitin', in talkin', seein' what kind of man you was.

MANOAH And what have you concluded?

MARSHAL I reckon you make a convincin' priest. Not surprised you got away with it so long.

Silence.

How about you put that shooter down and we can talk calmly?

MANOAH Will you lower your weapon?

MARSHAL I'll lower it, but I'm keepin' it to hand. If I wanted to shoot you I'd have just walked in here and done it. Just don't try nothin' foolish.

MANOAH *puts the shotgun on the altar.*

Step away from it…

MANOAH *walks away. The* **MARSHAL** *collects the shotgun.*

That's a fine weapon. You keep a loaded shotgun 'neath the altar?

MANOAH You never know who's gonna walk in.

MARSHAL Wise thinkin'.

MANOAH Are you going to arrest me?

MARSHAL We'll come to that. For now, I wanna talk.

MANOAH Take me in and I'll tell you everything you want to know.

MARSHAL I take you in and you're gonna be the main attraction, everyone's gonna want a piece of you – the infamous Jack Mason. I want to talk first, Jack.

MANOAH Please don't call me that.

MARSHAL Why not?

MANOAH Jack died fifteen years ago. I'm a different man.

MARSHAL Yeah, like you said, there was a boy who looked like you…

MANOAH But that's not me.

MARSHAL So what you want me to call you?

MANOAH Father. Or padre.

MARSHAL You ain't no priest.

MANOAH I've been a priest for fifteen years.

MARSHAL You may wear the clothes but that don't make you a priest.

MANOAH What does?

MARSHAL I dunno…

MANOAH I've cared for the people in these valleys for fifteen years. For fifteen years they have come to me for guidance and I have offered it to them, as their pastor. What else if that don't make me a priest?

No response.

Please, call me padre.

MARSHAL Alright, padre. I don't wanna know 'bout the last fifteen years, we'll get to that. I want to know what happened at La Muerte Negro.

MANOAH What do you want to know?

MARSHAL How you escaped. How you killed them people.

MANOAH Before I tell you, I want you to answer a question of mine.

MARSHAL I'm askin' the questions.

MANOAH I think it's the least you can do.

MARSHAL You answer my questions, then maybe I'll answer some of yours. Agreed?

MANOAH Agreed.

MARSHAL How did you escape that night?

MANOAH On foot.

MARSHAL You was tied to a barrel right down in the mines. How d'you escape?

MANOAH I managed to break from my ties.

MARSHAL You couldn't see, how d'you find your way out of the mines?

MANOAH The wind. It was summer, there was a hot wind blowing, just like today. It caught in the tunnels and forced its way right through the mine. I could feel it, you see, on my skin. Couldn't have been much more that a soft breeze by the time it made its way in, but I felt it strong enough. I followed it all the way down. I was half sure I was just getting lost. But I kept going, further and further. Then the path changed and started rolling uphill. The wind was stronger too – like it was rushing to get out just as I was. So I followed it up that slope until I reached the entrance.

MARSHAL You followed the wind? What if you'd got lost down there? In the dark, not able to see?

MANOAH That place was rigged to blow the next morning. As I saw it, there was no loss in trying.

MARSHAL No.

MANOAH But I made sure I could find my way back.

MARSHAL How?

MANOAH When I was a little boy, Leon told me the story of Theseus and the Minotaur. Do you know it?

MARSHAL I was also told it as a boy.

MANOAH When Theseus entered the labyrinth he carried a ball of string which unravelled and marked his way out of the tunnels.

MARSHAL You happened to have a ball of string down there with you?

MANOAH Not string, no. Plenty of fuse wire though.

MARSHAL You rewired the dynamite...

MANOAH Now I want to ask a question. When that dynamite went up and the mine came down, Jack Mason died; I never once used that name again, not even when I was alone. I don't reckon anyone's given him a second thought. Except you, marshal. So please, tell me, why have you tracked me all these years? Why didn't you believe I was dead?

MARSHAL Call it a gut feelin'. I just knew.

MANOAH You just knew?

MARSHAL Yeah, I just knew. I knew there weren't no way in hell my big brother would be so stupid as to let himself get buried in some shitty mine down in Mexico.

Silence.

MANOAH I see. You're the boy who was out playing at the creek...

MARSHAL Yeah.

MANOAH Eleven years old.

MARSHAL I guess my voice has changed somewhat.

MANOAH It has. Of course. Little Peter all grown up.

MARSHAL Yeah.

MANOAH You actually a marshal?

MARSHAL Sure am.

MANOAH If father could see you know.

MARSHAL He can't. You killed him that night.

Silence.

MANOAH I'm glad you went straight.

MARSHAL Even though it's given me the power to come find you?

MANOAH Even.

Silence.

I'm glad you're here, Peter. Truly, I am. I have thought on you over the years – wondered what you'd become. I'm glad to know you've turned out this way.

MARSHAL You don't know nothin' about me.

MANOAH No. Perhaps I'll get the chance?

MARSHAL Fact I'm your brother don't change anythin', Jack. I've come here for justice.

MANOAH Of course.

MARSHAL Did you know when you lit that fuse what would happen?

MANOAH I knew the mine would blow.

MARSHAL What about the camp? Huh?

Silence.

Did you know that the whole mountain would come down on that camp?

MANOAH No.

MARSHAL Did you know our ma was there? Our whole family was in that camp. Did you know that? Or did you just not care no more?

MANOAH I just lit the fuse, Peter.

MARSHAL You murdered the whole gang, Jack. You killed our whole family.

MANOAH I just lit the fuse. I didn't know what happened until you showed up here today and told me they were all dead. I swear, I didn't know.

Silence.

The **MARSHAL** *composes himself.*

MARSHAL What happened after you lit the fuse?

Pause.

MANOAH I left. I put my back against the mountain and just walked out, hoping I'd find my way to safety.

MARSHAL Miracle you wasn't killed, runnin' around in the dark with no eyes to see by.

MANOAH I was fortunate.

MARSHAL Did you hear the explosion?

MANOAH I did.

MARSHAL What did you feel? Relieved? Elated?

MANOAH Petrified. I couldn't tell how far I was, where I was headed, I couldn't see. In the darkness all I knew was I was alone in the world without even a friend to turn to. The explosion was louder than I ever could have imagined.

MARSHAL I heard it too.

MANOAH Of course. Wasn't that scared me so much as the silence that followed.

MARSHAL You were fortunate. It weren't silence where I was. When I ran back from that creek all I could hear was the screams from underneath. They didn't all die right away, Jack. Some of them was trapped – trapped under the rock with no air and no light to see by. I was eleven years old and I was alone, standin' on the edge of a rockslide with my whole family crushed and suffocatin' underneath. Buried alive.

MANOAH I'm sorry.

MARSHAL I started diggin', tryin' get some of them out. Time I got through to the first of 'em they'd swallowed that soil right into their lungs. Time the sun came up I'd pulled out over half a dozen of 'em. Never did find ma – she's still there, buried alongside a bunch of gunmen, miners and whores. I'd take your memory of silence over that any day.

MANOAH Yes.

Silence.

MARSHAL So you got away. How'd d'you end up here in the chapel of the martyr?

MANOAH I walked for what felt like weeks. When I fell I'd crawl. My hands and feet where nothing but blood and grit. I thought I was gonna die. When the sun was up I tried to sleep in whatever shade I could find. But the fever was strong and sleep was almost impossible. When the sun went down I would move, crawling mostly, trying to keep warm.

MARSHAL I get the picture.

MANOAH Eventually, I gave up hope. I lay there in the hot sun, baking like a corpse, flies swarming on me, crows coming down and picking at my flesh. Then the wind came again, and I heard it.

MARSHAL Heard what?

MANOAH The bell. The wind caught the chapel bell and it rang out, loud and clear. So I climbed onto my feet and I followed that sound 'til I hit the wall. I made my way inside and called out. The place was empty so I took it for shelter. There was tinned food and a well out the back for water. A few days passed and no one returned. In the wardrobe in the back room I found the cassocks – almost a perfect fit. I waited for days, ready to explain myself when the pastor returned, but he never did. I took it as a sign, Peter, a sign from God. I was going to die out there – but this chapel appeared for me, it saved me.

MARSHAL Horseshit.

MANOAH I understand you're not a God fearing man. And neither was I. But God saved me. Jack was dead, and I was reborn.

MARSHAL You know that ain't gonna save you now?

MANOAH I know.

MARSHAL Like I said, Jack, a man must be judged by his actions. If what you say is true, if you really ain't the man you was back then, if you believe different, then that's a shame – coz you still have to die.

MANOAH You sound like Leon.

MARSHAL No. I ain't like Leon, you saw to that.

MANOAH I wanted to protect you from him.

MARSHAL You up and left, Jack. How was you supposed to protect me from him when you weren't around no more? Huh?

MANOAH I was selfish. I can see that now.

MARSHAL I've heard enough.

MANOAH Remember that day down in San Sebastian? Remember how I tried to shield you from it all?

MARSHAL Well it was too late by then, weren't it? I was already part of the gang. I'd grown up watching my big brother Jack becomin' a gun slingin' legend and I wanted to be just like him. You may have had a change of heart, but not in time to save me.

MANOAH Yet here you are, a U.S. Marshal. You've become a better man than any of us. You're free of Leon and the Venenos.

MARSHAL I'll never be free of Leon. No one leaves the Venenos, Jack, you know that.

MANOAH I know you want your justice. But it don't have to be like this.

MARSHAL You ain't gonna beg for your life, are you? Jack Mason would never beg for his life.

MANOAH I'm not... No, I'll not beg.

MARSHAL You want to make your peace with God?

MANOAH I made my peace many years ago.

MARSHAL Then we best get on with it.

MANOAH What's your intention?

MARSHAL I mean to finish what was started all them years ago.

The **MARSHAL** *lifts the wooden crate onto the altar.*

Seems only right that this ends the way it began. I reckon Leon would like that – it would appeal to his sense of the theatrical.

MANOAH I reckon you're right.

MARSHAL Anythin' you want to say?

Silence.

MANOAH Will you bury me? I want the headstone to read 'Manoah'. Please, mark the grave for the priest who has served here for fifteen years. Will you do that?

Silence.

MARSHAL I'll bury you. But there ain't gonna be no markin'. I want you to rot in the ground in an unmarked grave – just like mother has done for all this time.

Silence.

Is that it?

MANOAH It is.

The **MARSHAL** *thumps heavily on the crate – from inside we hear a distinct rattle. He opens a hatch on the side of the box and steps away to the other side, leaving a clear line between* **MANOAH** *and the box. His gun is held ready.*

Do you know what became of Elena?

MARSHAL Leon gave her to a Mexican whorehouse.

MANOAH But he'd promised her amnesty?

MARSHAL Leon never was a man of his word. They advertised her as the wife of the late Jack Mason, the young fella who'd taken so many lives south of the border. People sure was willin' to take their revenge on her. I heard she died down there some years back from the fever.

Silence.

MANOAH Perhaps now I'll get to see her again.

MARSHAL You'll have all eternity to search for her through the nine circles of hell.

MANOAH *laughs.*

Now uncover your arm and step forward.

MANOAH *slowly walks towards the altar. His hands find the crate. He pulls back the robe from his right arm and takes a deep breath.*

MANOAH It's written in the Bible, 'Beloved, never avenge yourselves, but leave it to the wrath of the

Lord, for it is written, 'Vengeance is mine, I will repay."

MARSHAL Are you afraid to die?

MANOAH No.

MARSHAL Then quit talkin', Jack, coz I'm tired of this. Today… vengeance is mine. God will just have to wait.

MANOAH nods slowly. He pushes his arm through the open hatch into the crate. The rattle builds, fiercer and fiercer and then – darkness. From the shadows, ELENA's voice emerges.

ELENA
IN THE COLD AND DARK OF WINTER
I JOURNEYED FAR TO SEE MY LOVE.
EVERY DROP OF SNOW WOULD LINGER,
A PAINFUL JEST FROM HIM ABOVE.

JACK MANSON's voice joins her in the song.

BOTH
THE WHITE LAELIA GREW ABOUT HIM,
IT STOOD SO PROUD, ALONE AND BRAVE,
UPON THE TREES AMONG THE FOREST,
UPON THE TREES ABOVE HIS GRAVE.
IN THE GROUND BELOW THE MOUNTAINS,
HE HAD LAIN FOR THIRTEEN YEARS,
BUT COME THE WINTER I WOULD JOURNEY
TO WARM HIS TOMB WITH FALLING TEARS.

Finally, LEON's and PETER's voices join them.

ALL
THE WHITE LAELIA GREW ABOUT HIM,
IT STOOD SO PROUD, ALONE AND BRAVE,
UPON THE TREES AMONG THE FOREST,
UPON THE TREES ABOVE HIS GRAVE.

The End

Noche De Sangre

A short story sequel to
Blood Red Moon

The morning sun broke through the slatted carriage walls as the train tore across the dusty open plains, headed east. Rocking back and forth, the gentle percussion of the locomotive on the tracks would have put young Elijah Hill into a deep slumber, had it not been for the overwhelming stench of pigs swill and shit.

"You gonna hurl?" asked Isabel from across the carriage.

Elijah shook his head, though his pallid, sweat soaked brow betrayed him. The majority of the compartment was allocated to the pigs, whose filth filled the carriage with a rancid odor and mixed with the oppressive summer heat. At Elijah's end, apple boxes and supplies were piled high; between the seemingly endless crates the two sat, stretched out on bedrolls, having made a temporary home for themselves.

They had found each other at a small crossroads train station some days west of their current location. Isabel couldn't have been more than twenty years old, Elijah deduced from her unweathered skin and youthful stature. Elijah himself was not yet twenty one, but even so, he felt like a child when she spoke to him; despite her appearance, Isabel talked with a voice soaked in experience and wisdom. Her clothes were frayed and bleached from the sun and she didn't dress as the girls Elijah had known at home; she wore leather boots, thick suede trousers and a heavy plaid shirt. Padding, made from an old neckerchief, spilled from inside the rust colored leather hat that would have looked more at home on a cowboy than the girl who sat before him.

By comparison, Elijah's attire made him appear well bred and well moneyed. In truth, he had come from little money, his mother and father had farmed tobacco and made little more than enough to sustain the three of them. Upon their death, the sale of the farm and the house had secured sufficient finance to clear the debts arisen from their medical bills, to see them properly buried, and just enough, if well managed, to cover Elijah's journey east. If he had not crossed paths with the girl, he would not have been stowed away in a cargo compartment but would have been riding in far greater comfort towards the front of the train.

In the days since Isabel and Elijah climbed into their less than humble accommodation, she had shared little of her past. Elijah knew her to be a thief, a petty outlaw living hand to mouth, not at the misfortune, but the inconvenience of others. Perhaps it was this that aged her beyond her years, the ability to remain silent. Elijah, on the other hand, found the silence that often fell between them to be uncomfortable and would attempt to fill it with his own tale. She responded little, but she hadn't asked him to desist, so he continued to share every detail of his life so long as it passed the time.

Occasionally he wished he would stop talking, that he might be able to muster her level of patience, but soon enough the silence became deafening and his voice would resume its flow.

"Fore my mother died she was ramblin' and mutterin' in her sleep – talkin' to a fella named Enoch – beggin' forgiveness," Elijah spoke almost to himself, but under the tipped brow of her hat, Isabel listened closely. "I asked my pa what she was talkin' 'bout but he dismissed it as the fever, boilin' her brain, makin' her not talk sense. 'Cept she kept talkin' to this Enoch, so one day I tell her I'm Enoch and what's she got to be sorry for. I don't know if she was awake or asleep or what but she tells me how sorry she is for endin' my life and takin' the child and raisin' it without his real daddy."

Isabel lifted her head ever so slightly, not so as to reveal her eyes to the boy, but enough that demonstrated her interest in Elijah's story.

"Day we buried her I turned to my pa and I asked him straight out. He didn't deny it. He didn't say nothin' for some time. Just walked away and kept quiet about it.

I knew then there was truth to it. That night he came to me and told me everythin'. The fella who raised me, who I called 'Pa' was my uncle."

"Does that matter?" it was the first time Isabel had really acknowledged she was listening.

"No. Far as I'm concerned the man who raised me was my father – he took care of me and my ma for nineteen years since I was born, don't matter if we weren't blood, we was kin."

"Was?"

"Fever took him same winter it took my ma. Truth is, I reckon once she'd gone, it was just a matter of time 'fore he followed. Before he died he told me I have family back in Richmond, a grandmother."

"So that's where you're goin' now", everything she said sounded almost as if she was mocking him; Elijah took no offence but took it to be the way she spoke to everyone, with a sneer that gave her the sound of an old cowboy propping up a saloon bar rather than a girl of twenty years.

"Says they kept it from me all these years so as I wouldn't know who he was, wouldn't know what he done." She was the first person he'd spoken to on this subject since his father died; he felt a great relief in speaking it out loud.

"Who?"

"The man who sired me, he weren't a decent fella. My ma was worried that it runs in the blood, that if I knew what was in my blood maybe I'd turn out rotten just the same."

"You believe that?" The sneer cut through to Elijah this time, making him feel ashamed for his mother's foolishness.

"Of course not," he responded aggressively.

"Why o' course not?"

"You believe it?" He couldn't decide if he was being mocked.

"I once heard a story 'bout a wolf and a shaman," it was the most she'd spoken since they boarded the train; it relaxed Elijah and, though he was unsure what to make of the girl, he was glad for the company. "You know what a shaman is?"

"A witch doctor."

'The wolf is tired of his life on all fours, huntin' in the dirt," Isabel recounted the story as if she had done so a thousand times before. "And one day the wolf discovers the shaman by a camp fire, and he asks the shaman to –"

"The wolf speaks?" Elijah interrupted.

"Ain't you never heard a story before? The wolf asks the shaman to grant him a wish and turn him into a man so he can walk on two legs, can live in a house, sleep in a bed. Before granting the wish and casting the spell into the fire the shaman asks the wolf if he truly wants to be a man, if he truly believes he can change. Of course the wolf believes he can – the enchantment is made and the wolf lays down to sleep. On waking, he sees he is no longer a wolf, but a man. He thanks the shaman and journeys into town, rents a room, eats a fine meal and sleeps in a fine feather bed."

"And then what?"

"The shaman arrives and asks the wolf if he is happy as a man, if he has truly changed – the wolf says he has. The shaman decides to show the wolf around the town, to show him where he now lives. Leaving the hotel, the shaman leads the wolf to a farm where sheep are grazing in the field. The wolf cannot control himself, he falls to the ground on all fours, charges at the sheep and sinks his teeth into one of their necks. In that moment, as blood spills from the animal, the shaman overturns the enchantment and the wolf takes his true form once more, only to be discovered by the farmer and shot dead with his rifle."

"That's it?" Elijah's dissatisfaction was clear. "What's that supposed to mean?"

"Means we are what we was born to be", Isabel explained with no emotion or apparent care for the cruelty of the words she spoke. "Can't change that no matter how hard you try or how much you want it."

Elijah didn't offer a response. His mother had instilled in him so many traits he considered valuable, the desire to achieve, the desire to help others, the desire to make a difference. Yet he now learned the secret fear she'd held that underpinned these moral objectives; on reflection he was concerned by what chance he had of achieving them. *Perhaps she merely hoped to distract me from the life I was meant to live,* he worried.

The high pitched whistle of the steam engine broke the impending silence with its fierce screech.

"Must be comin' up on Black Rock", Isabel informed. The two collected their bedrolls and belongings and hid themselves behind a stack of wooden crates in the corner of the carriage. If anyone from the railroad were to open the doors they'd have seen the pigs locked in their pens and nothing but stacks of supply crates piled high.

Isabel and Elijah had performed this routine at every stop and station since boarding the train in California. Each time the awkwardness of being pressed together into such a confined space and remaining silent for such a long period became more and more apparent. Elijah was sure he could feel a tension growing between them. *Perhaps she's getting' tired of my company,* he wondered to himself, considering parting ways at the next station and joining a train the following day – at least that way he could travel alongside the rest of the passengers without fear of being caught. He quickly dismissed the idea.

Over the stench of the pigs, Elijah could just make out the girl's scent as he nestled in close behind the crates; it wasn't perfumed or fragrant, but the earthy smell of sweat, dirt and leather. As the train came to a halt by the stationhouse in Black Rock, the boy realized the comfort the smell brought to him. It had been some days since he'd last washed or changed his clothes; in that moment he hoped desperately that his own aroma was neither vile nor displeasing to his young traveling companion.

Elijah woke with a violent pain in his neck. From the rocking of the carriage he knew the train to be moving once again. He'd fallen asleep in their hold behind the crates with his head dropped sharply forward to his chest as he slumbered; his neck, stretched out like old rope, now felt reluctant to return to its correct position.

He lifted a hand to massage the afflicted muscles only to discover Isabel's head resting gently on his shoulder where she too had fallen asleep. Her leather hat had dropped from her head as she slept, revealing a mane of mouse brown hair, crudely fixed in a knot as kinks and ringlets broke free from the tie.

Without the rim of the hat pulled down over her brow, without the curled lip and sneer she always wore, Elijah saw the young girl for what she was and felt the overwhelming urge to pull her closer to him, to hold her tightly as she slept. Knowing the scolding he would receive upon her waking, he thought better of it.

With a gentle shove from Elijah, Isabel righted herself, emitting an ungraceful grunt – momentarily confused to be waking in the semi-darkness of a moving train carriage. With one unhappy look at the boy, she retrieved her hat and returned it, covering her hair and eyes once more.

"We're movin' again," Elijah offered. She didn't respond. Elijah wasn't sure if he preferred the silent Isabel or the Isabel who told unpleasant stories about wolves and witch doctors.

"Who's back there?" a thick, heavy voice came from beyond the apple crates. Elijah shot Isabel a panicked look – she seemed unconcerned.

"Who's out *there*?" she responded, the mocking tone to her voice clearer than ever.

"A man with a gun pointed on you – ready to fire if you don't come out slow." The deliberate click of a hammer cocking echoed around the wooden carriage. Elijah could barely make out the sound over the deafening thud of his heartbeat pounding in his ears, but glancing back to Isabel he witnessed its source.

"Jesus Christ, what are you doin?" Elijah whispered fiercely at the girl, who held a cocked revolver in her hand, before she silenced him with a single look.

"There two of you back there?" the man called out.

"Two of us, both armed and ready to shoot if we have to," Isabel responded with such calm, Elijah could only wonder how often she'd found herself in such situations.

"Won't make a difference, girl. I've got the drop on you and we both know it," the man sounded confident. "How 'bout you slide them weapons out and then we'll talk peaceful – I ain't lookin' to shoot no lady."

"Good coz there ain't no lady back here," Isabel spoke with the wit and drawl of a seasoned gunslinger. Elijah had little desire to die cowering in the corner of a travelling pigsty.

"I'm comin' out," he called loudly to the man, his voice trembling. "I ain't armed, ain't no cause to shoot – I'm comin' out slow." With hands raised above his head, Elijah lifted himself from behind the crates, ignoring the curses from Isabel who grappled in vain to hold him back.

Stood face to face with the armed man, a mixture of relief and added fear swept over the boy. Glancing to the tin star that was pinned to the man's chest, Elijah knew he wasn't about to be shot, but knew the chances of ending the day locked in a cell had just risen tenfold.

"You can put your arms down, son", the man offered. "Just step over here out the way so I got a clear line on your lady friend."

"It's alright", the boy's voice steadying, "he ain't gonna shoot us. This fella's a lawman."

"That right?" Isabel laughed.

"Sure is", the man responded, "and as I said, I ain't lookin' to fire on no lady, so you just slide that shooter out real slow and we'll resolve this peaceful."

A long silence fell in the carriage until it was broken by the clear sound of the hammer being slowly released, the revolver being lowered to the floor and the scrape as it was pushed across the wooden boards beneath their feet.

Without the fear that had occupied Elijah as he revealed himself, Isabel lifted herself casually from behind the crates and scowled at the lawman.

"You're right," he responded to seeing her, "you ain't a lady, you're just a girl."

"Allow me to take up that six-shooter and we'll see how much a girl I am."

"Put your boot on it and kick it gently over to me," the lawman instructed. Reluctantly, Isabel followed the command, handing over their only weapon to the armed man who took it in his free hand and examined it. "That's a fine gun," he concluded, before lowering his own and returning it to the leather gun belt that hung on his hips. In one swift move the lawman spun Isabel's revolver so the polished wooden handle faced the girl. Releasing his grip, he lifted the weapon towards her in offer.

"This some kind of trick?" she questioned, her lips barely parting to allow the words to pass.

"No trick. My gun's holstered, you do the same with this one, then all three of us can return to journeyin' east in peace."

"You ain't gonna arrest us?" the relief in Elijah's voice was clear.

"I got bigger priorities, son," responded the lawman, a sense of amusement to his words. "I ain't lookin' to arrest a couple of kids for trespassin'. So once your girlfriend puts this peacemaker out of sight, I'm gonna open a crate of them apples in search of a somethin' ripe and delicious, stretch out on the floor away from them swine and shut my eyes."

Her eyes narrowed and her stance readied to tackle the lawman if needs be, Isabel retrieved her six-shooter. As promised, the lawman stepped away from the couple and as Isabel fixed the gun under her jacket, he began prying open one of the lids to reveal the fresh green apples beneath.

As the afternoon wore away, the three traveled in peace. Isabel, as always, kept to herself. Elijah had found in the lawman someone to fill the silence and monotony of the journey. Though he suspected that nine in every ten statements the man made were either untruthful or exaggerated, it was a welcome respite from his own voice.

"And I looked the dude dead in the eye," the lawman's story concluded, "and I says to him he best be sure he can shoot straight or he's gonna be eatin' lead for his dinner."

"What does he do?" Elijah humored him.

"He drops the gun to the dirt and I walk him right down Main Street and into a jail cell," a look in his eyes told the boy the lawman believed his story, no matter how untrue it was likely to be. "When those iron bars closed on him, the entire town comes out on their porches to applaud – they give me an ovation you could have heard right across the county."

Isabel let out a low, quiet laugh.

"Somethin' funny, little miss?" Elijah saw the lawman was on the verge of losing his temper – it wasn't the first response from the girl that had caught his attention.

"Nothing funny at all," her contempt for the man not even a little guarded.

"This kid tells me he's travelin' east to find his kin; how come you're ridin' the train, girl?"

"Coz I ain't got no place better to be," she retorted quickly. "What about you, lawman, how come you're hitchin' a ride in here with the pigs and not sitting in comfort 'longside the women?"

"I'm protectin' a load."

"Protectin' cargo?" Isabel laughed. "You mean you're takin' care of pigs? Ain't that farmhand's work?"

"It ain't the pigs I'm protectin'," the lawman didn't take kindly to being laughed at. "In the carriage next over is a safe containin' more gold than you could dream of."

"So why ain't you ridin' in the carriage next over?"

"'Coz that's just what they'd expect", the lawman shared his plan, trying to impress the pair with his cunning.

"Who does the gold belong to?" Elijah enquired, trying to deflect the conversation from Isabel.

"The kind of fellas you don't steal from."

The sun was hanging low in the sky, soon to fall below the mountains to the north. The lawman's stories had come to an end, either through Elijah's waning interest, or the lawman's own boredom at the sound of his voice.

The three sat in silence, sprawled out about the carriage between the apple crates. To Elijah's relief, the evening was beginning to cool – the overwhelming stench of the animals beginning to fade. A heavy crash came from the wood overhead.

"Crows," the lawman informed Elijah, casually putting to rest the moment of fear that had startled him.

The boy's eyes relaxed, finding their place on Isabel, who slumped in the corner, hat pulled down, her hand constantly resting on the grip of her revolver. He wondered if the lawman would leave them, or if they'd depart the train at the next station. He wondered if, once they'd climbed from the carriage, whether they'd stay together, traveling east as a pair. They'd known each other only a few days, but the thought of journeying on alone filled Elijah with an unease, or perhaps a sadness.

The deep orange glow of the setting sun poured through the carriage; a comforting light that transported Elijah to his parents' tobacco farm back home. *No longer theirs,* he realized as he pictured the simple wooden house with its heavy stone chimney, a constant stream of smoke rising into the still air. The cruel odor of his accommodation aboard the train departed slowly, shifting into the sweet, all too familiar scent of the tobacco crop, almost roasting in the hot Californian sun. He'd never known anywhere else, and the thought of the house now the property of a stranger left a sickness in his gut, but for a moment he returned, walking waist-deep through the endless rows of green plants. He could see his mother, sewing on the front porch. Beyond her, his father, singing as he worked, *'Close down the fire, sister.'* Elijah knew the tune and the words by heart. His parents never told him its significance, but when his father sang that song his mother's smile would broaden and seemingly never depart.

Apples scattered through the carriage as crates tumbled to the floor, splitting on the wooden boards. Elijah woke as the world around him evaporated and he found himself being dragged violently from his perch. He looked to see who had taken hold of him, thinking them to have been discovered by a railroad man, but there were no hands on him.

The pull subsided as the train's abrupt halt came to an end – its whistle blowing fiercely. Elijah, panicked, looked about through the evening light to his traveling companions. Isabel, crouched but upright, held her six-shooter tight in her grasp. The lawman, like Elijah, looked confused and startled as he awkwardly lifted himself, searching for an explanation.

"What in Jesus Christ's name was that?" he hissed.

"Train's stopped", Isabel wasted no time with her words.

"We ain't scheduled to stop 'til mornin'."

"This ain't a scheduled stop," she dropped her eyes pointedly to the gun on his hip.

"Oh Jesus," he drew the gun, his mind finally caught up with the situation.

"What are we gonna do?" Elijah's heart was pounding through his entire body.

"We're gonna wait," the lawman decided. "We're just gonna sit tight and wait this out."

"Some lawman you are," vitriol spewed from Isabel's glare. "There's innocent people up there, you gonna leave them to fend for themselves?"

"I don't know how many there is of them. If I go out guns blazin' before I know the score there's gonna be plenty more dead, myself included." His logic seemed sound, though the fear behind his eyes betrayed his true motivations.

"You're a goddamn coward," Isabel calmly informed him.

"I don't see you racin' out there," the lawman could barely meet her eyes.

"You two best stop this," Elijah found his voice. "If there's trouble out there, we don't need none in here."

"You gotta do somethin'", Isabel's voice was stern.

"I count at least a half dozen", no matter how sternly Isabel may have spoken, it was not going to convince the lawman. "I ain't goin' out there one against six."

"There's three of us."

"There's two of us with guns," he corrected her, "And I ain't never seen you shoot."

"Don't look like I'll ever see *you* shoot. You even fired that gun in the name of justice?"

"Them fellas who own that gold," he began to explain, "They paid a fee for safe passage but I ain't gonna get myself killed over other men's gold."

Elijah looked through the slatted wall as the gang approached the rear of the train. With one man left to watch over the passengers, the rest of them, six men, prepared to blast open the safe. A charge of dynamite secured to the metal vault, a length of fuse wire was rolled out to a comfortable distance.

"In your own time," drawled a man, clearly the group's leader. Dark, jaundiced eyes piercing through weathered, leather skin behind a red, stained bandana.

The carriages rocked on the tracks as the explosion carried through the train. Elijah had never heard a noise so loud, like a thousand claps of thunder rolled into one. His ears whined and whistled and for a moment the world fell silent.

The outlaws cheered as the smoke cleared, revealing the broken safe and, amidst the ruins, a dozen heavy gold bars. Each heavy enough for one man to struggle with its weight and marked on each, a symbol, three letters, 'APR'.

"Now's your chance," whispered Isabel inside the next carriage. "They're distracted; you can get the drop on 'em easy." The lawman did not respond. "Well Jesus! If you won't…"

She reached for the handle of the compartment door, her other hand still tightly gripped to her revolver.

"No!" before Isabel had made contact with the metal handle, she found herself pulled forcefully to the ground, the lawman's hand on the back of her neck.

To the men outside, despite their attention being fixed firmly on their newfound wealth, there was no mistaking the sound.

"Who's in there?" called the leader. Panicked eyes searched through the ever darkening carriage as the three considered a way out of their predicament. "I know someone's in there. I ain't dumb. I ain't deaf, neither."

"I don't mean no harm," the lawman's voice was filled with fear as he called out.

"What you doin' in there with the animals?"

"Just hitchin' a ride," Isabel watched the lawman as he offered his feeble excuses.

"You're gonna open that door and come out real slow," the bandit instructed. "You got a weapon?" The lawman thought for a moment, before quietly discarding his firearm in the shadows.

"No, I ain't armed."

"It just you in there?"

Isabel gave the man a nod of clear instruction.

"It is," the lawman responded. "It's just me."

"Then come out, real slow." Elijah and Isabel moved away from the doors, out of sight. Elijah pressed his face to a gap in the boarded wall. Through the crack in the wood he could see the men, guns in hand, ready and waiting. He'd never seen men like them before, but he'd heard enough stories to know their kind. Men of bad blood, the kind that had run in his grandfather's, his father's, and now in his own.

The door creaked heavily as it rolled open, scraping across the metal frame. The deep, orange sunlight flooded the carriage; there was still much more day than it had appeared to Elijah inside the dark train car.

His hands open palmed, fingertips to the sky, the lawman edged forward.

"Climb down," came the next instruction. The lawman did as told. He looked in that moment to Elijah as a child, misbehaved and now remorseful of his ill-advised actions. "What you doin' hidin' in there?"

"Nothin'", the lawman's voice trembling uncontrollably. "I was just stealin' a ride."

"Stealin', was you?" the leader was clearly entertained. "Why is it you think I ain't so quick in believin' your story?"

"It's the truth, I swear."

"Don't lie to me," the humour was fading from the bandit's voice.

"I ain't lyin'".

"You say you're just stowed away for a ride? How come you got a tin star pinned to your chest?" a smile cracked across the bandit's face as the realization dawned on the lawman. "Huh, marshal?"

"I... I ain't –" the lawman spluttered.

"You ain't a marshal? You're wearin' the badge. You know what I think," the bandit explained, "is that you been put here by APR, but when it came down to it you're too chicken shit. You got the badge on the outside, but inside you're yeller. Sound about right?"

"I don't want no trouble", tears streamed down the coward's face, marking lines through his dirt stained skin.

"Then you won't get none", smiled the gang leader. "You just take off that badge, drop it to the dust, and far as I'm concerned, you ain't a lawman no more."

Fumbling with the metal pin, the lawman pulled the star from his chest and threw it to the ground.

"There," he announced, pathetically, "like you says, I ain't a lawman no more."

"Exactly," the bandit grinned; his men chuckling at the feeble, cowardly scene.

"I mean it", confirmed the coward, "I ain't a lawman."

"That's good", the bandito grinned wider than ever. "That's real good, 'cause you get in awful trouble for killin' a lawman." With a steady, single movement, the bandit pulled his gun right between the man's eyes. Blood and brains crashed through the lawman's shattered skull as a solitary round erupted from the outlaw's forty-four.

Elijah recoiled in shock from the sight and sound of his former travelling companion's execution. He made hardly a movement, but it was enough for the bandit to glimpse through the crack in the wood.

"I see you", he spoke out, calmly. "I see you in there. And I'm gonna give you to the count o' ten to step out with your palms to God."

Isabel shot the boy an angry glare. He felt so foolish and cowardly to have put them both in danger.

The bandit called out the count, his men taking aim at the doors once more. Elijah, with the attempted appearance of bravery, made to stand up, walk towards the carriage door and step out into the sunset. As he began to lift himself to his feet, a forceful hand pulled him back into the shadows. Isabel shook her head.

"You stay here," she whispered, before thrusting her revolver beneath the cover of her jacket and calling out loudly to the bandits, "I'm comin' out!" The boy didn't know what to do; he could have stepped out alone and they would never have known Isabel was hidden inside.

"That a girl in there?" called the bandit.

"That's right, just a girl. No need for shootin'. Hear me?"

As she walked out in front of the doors, the deep sunlit glow caught her, giving her skin a softness that Elijah observed as he looked on in both terror and disbelief.

Elijah did not dare put his face to the cracks in case he give himself away once more. He sunk into the darkness, crouched low beside the apple crates, and listened to the conversation between Isabel and the gang. She spoke so calmly, not as the lawman had done, but as someone unafraid to die. Elijah knew if he were out there he would not have handled himself nearly so well.

"You a lawman as well, little girl?" the bandit laughed.

"Just a stowaway."

"That's just what your friend here said, right 'fore I shot him."

"He weren't my friend," she retorted. "That dude was a coward."

"He deserve what he got?" the bandit clearly found great entertainment in the girl's spirited attitude. As did his men who watched the scene, relaxed, guns by their sides.

"He was a lawman, weren't he?" It was almost more than Elijah had heard her speak in the days since they met. "Man's job was to protect the train and the people on it

from fellas like you. He should have come out shootin'
and taken some of you sons of bitches down 'fore he hit
the dirt."

"Is that so?" the bandit was growing increasingly amused.

"That's so."

"You so sure of yourself, maybe you should be a lawman
after all." Elijah waited through a long silence as the gang
leader collected the tin star from the dirt and pinned
it to Isabel's jacket. "There you go, you look just the
part."

"Ain't you gonna give me a gun?" the girl laughed with
the man.

"Afraid not," the bandito laughed harder.

"That's alright," came Isabel's calm response as a
hand darted beneath her jacket and, quick as lightning,
returned with a peacemaker that took its aim right
between the laughing man's eyes. "I got my own."

To the sound of guns lifting through the air, and
hammers cocking, Elijah shifted himself to peer through
the carriage wall. As he moved, his hand brushed
something heavy and metallic on the floor.

Outside, Isabel's aim was held firm on the bandit. On
Isabel, five barrels took their own aim. *What the hell is she
doing?* Elijah couldn't believe what he saw. He couldn't
envisage a way out of this situation in which Isabel could
possibly survive. Sure she had her gun on the boss, but if
she were to fire, her one bullet would be met with their
five.

Elijah felt for the heavy metal object beneath him.
At least I can shift the odds in her favor, he thought, lifting
himself towards the door.

Isabel heard the hammer cock behind her and, for a
brief moment, worried she'd been out maneuvered.

"That you, Elijah?" she questioned.

"Yeah," his reply was breathy, tense; sweat dripped from
his palms.

"Seems we got ourselves a situation," the bandit's voice
now entirely devoid of humor.

"There's no situation," Isabel appeared totally in control. "Your boys are gonna put down their guns, lay down in the dirt and put their hands behind their backs. Me and my boy are gonna take a couple of your horses and ride off. We're all gonna keep calm, keep our heads, and there's no situation."

"We're just gonna let you ride off?" Elijah could see the man wanted nothing more than to pull his gun and end her right there.

"You ain't lettin' us do nothin'," she explained. "I'm tellin' you what you're gonna do."

"And if I don't want to?"

"Then I'm gonna shoot you, your boys is gonna shoot me, and my boy up there is gonna shoot all of them."

"That so?" the bandit laughed; Elijah was sure he could sense the bluff.

"Sure is," Isabel maintained the ruse with complete conviction. "The boy's a regular Jack Mason with a peacemaker."

"That right, son?" the bandit offered to Elijah, whose hands were beginning to tremble. But before he could open his mouth it was Isabel who answered.

"You're damn right it is. And my guess is you ain't willin' to bet your life on it bein' any other way."

A long, uncomfortable silence fell between the group. Elijah could feel a pain, burning beneath his arms from the weight of the gun as the outlaws, Elijah and Isabel waited for their potential end in the dying light of the sun.

Finally, the bandit spoke.

"Alright," his voice was quiet and full of rage; he clearly wanted the young girl dead, but wasn't willing to risk taking a bullet himself. "Boys, do as the young lady lawman says. Guns down. Faces down. Hands behind your backs."

Slowly, and with clear reluctance, the men did as instructed. Isabel kept her sights aimed right on the leader, without so much as a blink.

"You put yours down, an' all," she instructed and the bandit did as he was told. "And kick it away. Now get down on your knees, hands on top of your head."

"Ain't you gonna have me lyin' in the dirt?" a slight sense of amusement crept across his face.

"I want you to be able to see us when we go ridin' off on your horses."

"What's to stop us ridin' after you?"

"We got ourselves a deal, ain't we?" she spoke with such confidence, as though the man wasn't threatening to kill her. "You comin' after us is gonna be in direct contravention of that deal, ain't it."

The bandit didn't offer a response, but simply smiled a crooked smile and held the girl's gaze without blinking.

"Hey, gunslinger," she called up to Elijah. "Pick up these gentlemen's weapons, throw 'em in with the pigs. Then go fetch us two of them horses."

The sun's warmth was a distant memory by the time Isabel and Elijah arrived at the town. The moon was high in the night sky; the path was perfectly illuminated in its cold, bright light. They'd taken some twists and turns along the way, doubled back and rode half a mile down a shallow creek with the hope of making it harder for the bandits, if they did decide to follow.

The town was no more than a single street, lined on each side with simple wooden buildings. Two saloons marked each end, between them a grocer's store, a livery, a tailor's, a few run down houses and in the center of town, a hotel. In the distance, a chapel sat atop a hill, overlooking it all.

Much to Elijah's irritation Isabel had spoken barely a word since they parted the railroad. He still couldn't comprehend the situation they had not only survived, but won. He wanted nothing more than to talk with the girl, to give her thanks for saving them both. But she said nothing and so he too remained silent.

With the horses fed, watered, and secured at the livery, the young traveling companions booked two rooms at the hotel. Elijah paid for them both, looking worriedly at his ever dwindling supply of coin.

"Goodnight," he offered as they parted ways at the top of the stairs – her room was a little further along the landing. Elijah stopped awkwardly, with his bedroll and bag under each arm, and eventually offered his thanks.

"I weren't savin' you," she responded as she made her way towards her room, struggling under the weight of her own luggage, the tin star still pinned to her jacket. "I was savin' myself. You're just an added bonus."

"Well you talked us out of it," he continued, finally able to share everything that had been on his mind the entire ride. "You talked us right out of there. That was all your thinkin', and it was your thinkin' to double back. There ain't no way they're gonna be able to find us now. You talked us out without shootin' and didn't give them no cause to follow. I swear, I ain't never seen somethin' so brave and clever all at the same time."

"Goodnight, Elijah," she offered impatiently, disappearing from the corridor into her room.

Inside his own, Elijah laid out his bed roll on the floor beneath the open window. One glance at the lice-ridden bed on the other side of the room was enough to make another night bunking on a hard wooden floor somehow seem appealing.

The thoughts of home that had occupied his mind the last time he had slept, what now felt like a lifetime ago, were long gone. His mind thought only on Isabel, on the incredible bravery she had shown, on her skill, intelligence and wit. But as the exhaustion of the day finally caught Elijah, he lay fully clothed on his roll and drifted away with only a single image to haunt his dreams – three letters, 'APR'.

The deafening blast of a gunshot woke Elijah, his entire body immobile, frozen in terror. Through the room he could just make out a figure, silhouetted in the doorway from the gas lamp burning in the hall. Smoke spun about him, seeping from the gun and mixing with the dust that had been shaken from the room by the blast.

Elijah tried to drag himself away into the shadows, to hide, to put any kind of distance between himself and the stranger, but his body simply would not move. As if paralyzed, he looked on as the figure entered the room and fumbled towards the bed.

Pulling back the sheets the man found nothing between them other than crawling lice and a single, smoking bullet hole. *It's only a matter of time 'fore he sees me,* panicked Elijah as the man turned to search the room.

Outside on the veranda that ran around the entire building, Elijah made out some footsteps, creaking against the wood. *That's it, I'm trapped,* he despaired, thinking there to be a second assailant just beyond the window.

As the second shot broke the night, Elijah was certain his life was over. Yet the sound of the gunfire was not met with his death, but with another sound. The assassin inside the room crumpled to the floor, gasping for breath as his lungs filled with blood. Elijah's eyes turned to the window where the smoking barrel of a forty-four was quickly joined by Isabel, climbing in through the open frame.

"That's the second time I've saved your ass," she informed him as she stepped over his immobile body, heading towards the writhing body beyond.

A long, heavy breath exhaled from the young boy as the realization swept across him.

"Where are the others?" Isabel interrogated the dying man. "Listen up dude, you're dyin'. Loyalty to them fellas ain't gonna do you no favors now. So you tell me where they're at."

Whether the man was opening his mouth to share his knowledge, or to offer one final curse to the girl who had ended his life, Isabel would never know, for all that emitted from between his pale, blue lips was a cough full of deep red blood.

Elijah had pulled himself to his feet, his heart pumping in his chest, hands and legs all at the same time.

"What the hell?" he exclaimed, barely able to breathe himself.

"They found us," Isabel explained, collecting the man's gun. "Grab your shooter and follow me." Before the boy had a moment to think, she was back out the window and heading along the gantry.

Elijah followed her along the outside of the building and up a small wooden ladder to the roof where she ducked down low and fixed her eyes on the street below.

"Rest of the gang will have heard them shots," there was fear in her voice; of all that had occurred that day, it was the sound of fear in Isabel that scared Elijah more than anything. "We need to get out," she continued. "We get out quick 'fore they realize what's happened."

"But where's the rest of 'em?" Elijah couldn't understand quickly enough. "Why'd they only send one o' them?"

"They sent two, one for each of us. I got 'em both – means there's five of them left out there. We need to get out."

"They tracked us all the way from the railroad," Elijah worried aloud. "We go out there and they'll hunt us down before the sun comes up."

Isabel drew a single finger to her lips and pointed to the street below. Elijah followed her gaze to the small group of men moving from the shadows of an alley across the way. As they stepped out into the moonlit night, Elijah watched the masked faces of the five men as they crossed the street and made their way inside the hotel.

"You got a better idea?" Isabel's fear was poorly disguised as anger.

"I don't know," Elijah wished he could be as clever as she was, that he could think their way out of this situation as she had done earlier. "I know if we go out there they'll be nowhere for us to hide. At least here we've got some cover."

"We ain't gonna hide up here all night."

"We've got guns," he thought aloud. "We wait 'til they come up here and we fight."

"Five against two? You ever fired a gun before?"

He buried his head in his hands, wracking his brains for some shred of an idea. He thought on the gang of bandits, on the people aboard the train, on the lawman whose corpse lay in the sand beside the tracks. It was in this last image that he recalled one useful grain of information.

"The tin star…" he realized.

"What?" Isabel didn't understand his meaning.

"The marshal's badge, give it to me." She unclipped the star from her jacket.

"What are you gonna do?" it was the first time since they'd met he felt she actually wanted him to answer.

'I'm gonna go to the saloon", he spoke the plan, concocting it just moments before it left his mouth. "I'm gonna tell 'em I'm a lawman and there's a gang of outlaws hidden in town and there's a reward – a bounty."

"You ain't got no money for a bounty."

"But the American Pacific Railroad has," he explained. "Did you see it on the gold, 'APR', that's who they was stealin' from. We get them the men who robbed their train and they'll pay a bounty alright."

"Fine", the girl conceded. "Go."

"You think it'll work?"

"We ain't got nothin' better."

The night was late and the saloon was filled only with drinkers well in their cups. A bunch of farm hands and cowboys at the end of their day's work, drinking their pay. *These fellas will have to do,* thought Elijah, as he pushed through the swinging doors into the gas lit bar.

The star hung heavy on his chest, the peacemaker on his hip, heavier still. Two steps in and he could feel the adrenaline pumping through his veins, his forehead slick with sweat. He stopped in his tracks, filled his lungs and puffed his chest.

"I'm formin' a posse", he announced feebly to the room. Most men ignored him, the barman watched him curiously.

"What you say, kid?" asked the innkeeper.

"I said", Elijah deepened his voice, attempting to fill it with more gravity, "I'm formin' a posse. There's a gang of railway thieves here in town. I need these fellas' assistance in bringing them to justice."

"You're a lawman?" the barman laughed. "You ain't hardly out of swaddling."

"I am a US Marshal" a flash of rage in the young man. "I'm offering a hundred dollars apiece for any man who helps me bring this gang to justice." The saloon fell quiet with the mention of money, every man's eyes fixed on the boy. "I may be young", Elijah continued, "but that is a fair offer for any man."

"Let me see that badge" called one of the drinkers. Elijah unclipped the star and handed it to him. "It's genuine" concluded the man.

"Now will you stop doubtin' me and start helpin'?" The room filled with whispers as the men hurriedly weighed up the cost. Elijah knew he had them. He collected the star, returning it to his chest, and headed for the door.

"Where you goin'?" called the barman.

"I'm walking out that door and goin' to find these men", he spoke casually and with the command of a lawman. "Any man with me by the time I step out onto the street will receive a hundred dollars. Any man who waits to finish his whiskey before joining us will receive only fifty."

With that, he pushed through the doors, letting them swing theatrically behind him. The saloon burst into action as almost each and every man jumped to their feet and bolted for the street.

By the time the posse had arrived outside the hotel, weapons in hand, blood pumping and fuelled for a gunfight, there was all but silence coming from the building. The candles and gas lamps had been extinguished, but the glow of the moonlight was enough to make out the figures, moving behind the windows.

"That's them", Elijah informed the men to his side. "There's five in total. There's a body in each of the north facin' rooms. We need to spread out, make sure there's no way out for 'em. There's a gantry on the roof, you can cross over to the buildings adjacent – let's put some fellas up there and all."

"You lookin' to take prisoners, marshal?" asked one of the men.

"No", Elijah decided. "I ain't."

As the townsmen headed out and surrounded the hotel, Elijah looked up to the rooftop. He couldn't see Isobel. He prayed that she was somewhere safe before realizing that he had no right nor need to protect her, it was she who had been taking care of him.

The noise of boots on soil and timber came to an end – the men were in position. Elijah had only planned to this point; the rest was unknown to him. He stepped forward, calling out to the men inside.

"There ain't no way you're comin' out shootin", he informed them. "We got the whole place covered. So there's only two ways this is gonna go down. The first; you're gonna hurl them guns out the windows and you're gonna walk out slow with your hands to the sky." He used the very same instructions the bandit had given them that very evening. "The second; you keep them guns, and we come take them from your dead bodies."

Even Elijah couldn't tell if he was bluffing. The marshal's badge on his chest, coupled with the posse of over a dozen men, gave him a strength he'd never felt. People respected him beyond his years, people trusted him.

"I'm gonna give you to the count of ten", he continued the routine he'd learned from the bandits themselves. "One. Two. Three." As his count reached seven, a familiar voice yelled out from inside.

"Alright", the gang leader called. "Alright, we're gonna do as you says."

Elijah couldn't believe it had worked. It was almost too easy – the simple power of the tin star.

A flash of lightning tore through the night sky – a gunshot. A cloud of dust billowed into the moonlight as a man to Elijah's left collapsed into the dirt. From inside the hotel a dozen shots rang out. The air filled with a hundred more as the posse, drunk and trigger happy, unleashed their fire.

The street filled with the thick smoke of gunpowder. As the walls splintered from the scatter of bullets, and the windows shattered, spraying shards of glass into the air, the outlaws burst from the hotel with eyes full of rage and bloodlust.

Bodies dropped on each side, but the numbers were in Elijah's favor, and soon the outlaws' guns fell silent, as their owners fell to the ground.

"Stop!" called Elijah over the deafening sound of the posse's roaring bullets. "That's enough!"

Smoking barrels held their aim as blood soaked into the dry desert ground – thick black pools emerging in the moonlight. Five bodies, lying in the dirt, torn through with lead.

Elijah stepped towards them, signaling for the posse to lower their guns. He made his way towards the gang's leader, a body writhing in a pool of blood.

The outlaw's lungs clawed at the night air, searching desperately for breath. His fingers scratching at his throat where a bullet had torn the flesh. A half decent doctor and this man might have lived, but the boy standing over him knew he couldn't allow that. This outlaw would have murdered Elijah and Isabel without so much as a moment's doubt – he couldn't let him live.

Elijah took aim between the man's eyes. In that moment he thought of his mother, of the principles she had instilled in him. *Was this helping others?* he thought. *Was this making a difference?* He could not tell where the line was drawn. He was about to take a man's life. With the star pinned over his heart, he was protected by the law, but was he any different from the man who sired him? He was about to take a life in cold blood; not for justice or honor, but simply to protect himself.

The revolver shook as his hand trembled. He pulled the lever back, the sound of metal against metal filling the silent, waiting street. The burden of the peacemaker felt immense in his grip. He wanted to walk away, to turn and run. But he knew what the men expected of him, they looked on, eyes full of bloodlust, desperate to witness this one final execution.

The tin star had saved Elijah from almost certain death, and now he knew he must repay it. A rage soared through his body; it was not the darkness that was bred into him, but the kindness that his mother had instilled, a disgust at the murder he was about to commit. He would repay the star that had saved his life, but not with blood, with justice.

Slowly, carefully, Elijah pushed the hammer forward, disarming the gun, and returned the peacemaker to his belt. A whisper of discontent spread about the waiting street as the bloodthirsty posse realized the lawman's decision.

"Get this man a doctor", Elijah announced to the crowd. "And call for the blacksmith to fasten him in irons."

In that moment the boy transformed; he became the man he would be for the rest of his life.

Elijah rose early the following morning, unable to sleep. The clouds that hung above the horizon caught the sunrise, turning the sky a violent shade of red. Sat on the gantry of the hotel, he looked down to the street where the ground was stained a darker shade than the sky above it.

On the steps below, unaware of Elijah watching on, Isabel sat, puffing on a cigarillo and gazing into the blood soaked earth.

Elijah had wondered where the girl had been as the fight broke out, whether she had looked on as he led the posse to bring down their attackers. He hoped desperately that she had seen every moment and was grateful for him and all he had done.

"It's a fine morning", he offered as he climbed down to meet her on the street.

"Sure is", she didn't turn to look at him, but kept her gaze fixed on the horizon.

"The red sky?" Elijah followed her eyes. "Means rain's comin'."

"I heard different."

"Yeah?"

"Heard the sky bleeds red when the sun rises after a night of bloodshed", she spoke as if she knew the words were untrue, but secretly wished there to be something in them.

"Why did they want us so bad?" Elijah tried to understand, his eyes lowered to the scarred earth before them. "Why didn't they just let us go?"

"I dunno", her gaze still fixed firmly on the rising sun.

"Sure we took a couple of horses", he continued. "But nothin' worth dyin' over."

"We took more than their horses."

"What d'you mean?" Elijah thought back to the events at the railway.

"Men like that" she explained. "They ain't about to let a kid and a girl get the better of them. We took their pride."

That afternoon, when the men arrived from the American Pacific Railroad, Elijah met them. He went to them not as the boy stowed away on their train, headed east without any real purpose, but as a young lawman, the man responsible, as they were concerned, for rescuing the stolen gold, and for bringing down an apparently notorious railroad gang.

Elijah escorted them to the livery where the outlaw had been treated by the doctor, and chained in a makeshift cell. The wound in his neck was well cleaned and bandaged, but his shirt was torn open to reveal a hole through his stomach where crude, late night surgery had failed to retrieve a second bullet. The hay beneath the outlaw was soaked in the dead man's blood.

Elijah looked down at the corpse of the man whose life he had spared but hours ago. With a sigh of relief, he knew he'd done the right thing, even if nature had taken her own course in the end.

The APR men did as Elijah had hoped; they paid each member of the posse a handsome reward for bringing down the gang of thieves and securing the gold.

Elijah was a hero in the small town, everyone knew him, they respected him. Alongside the handsome reward paid by the APR, a local official offered the young lawman a gift, an elegant gold pocket watch, which Elijah accepted gracefully, and kept tucked in his waistcoat. Isabel had watched on as he was praised and championed, laughing quietly from beneath the brow of her hat.

The night before, Elijah had waited for the bodies to be cleared, for the town to go to sleep, before he searched the gang's horses for the gold. Eleven bars in total, hidden within the saddlebags. Lifting them out one by one, he was amazed the horses had carried them all this way without their legs buckling under the weight.

After he led the APR men to the stash of gold they asked him how many he'd found.

"Just as you see 'em," he answered honestly. "Eleven. Ain't that all of them?"

"Almost". sneered one of the men, clearly the senior of the other two.

They searched the horses again and headed off towards the outlaws' tracks to continue their search in the direction of the train.

"I guess one of them bars must've got lost in the sand", he thought aloud.

"Guess so", Isabel offered as they sat that evening over a bottle of corn liquor in the hotel bar.

"Where you gonna go from here?"

"I don't know", Elijah had been thinking the same question all day. "Maybe I won't go anywhere. Reckon I might stay here a while."

"You gonna keep that thing on?" she pointed to the metal star.

"Thought I might", he confessed, smiling.

"Young Elijah Hill, the lawman", she teased him gently.

"It's as good a thing as any to do, I guess."

"Yeah" she eyed him closely. "Guess you ain't gonna turn out so bad after all."

"Guess not", he thought about his mother's words, of what she'd always encouraged him to believe in. "What about you? What you gonna do?"

"Head back to the tracks", she thought aloud, "Climb onto the next train comes through – keep headin' east. You reckon you'll get along alright without me to get you out of trouble?"

"Twice you got me out of danger", Elijah agreed.

"And once you got us out", she offered kindly.

"Guess that means I owe you."

"Guess so. I get to choose my reward?" she laughed.

"I reckon you got your reward already."

"How's that?"

"Eleven gold bars I found last night", he smiled. "The APR men seemed to think there was one missin'. Strange that. Don't you think?"

The girl smiled back, without saying a word.

The End

Property List

They check their guns. Felix carries a long barrelled revolver. Benjamin is armed with a peacemaker and a repeater rifle (p95)
Pocket watch (p104)
Two contracts (p105)
Glass of water (p107)
Pen (p114)
Shefiff's badge (p117)
Benjamin rifles through the contract and papers dropped by Lillian. He picks up the telegram and reads it (p124)
Manoah returns carrying a small wooden box... he pulls a pistol from the box (p133)

Volume III the Rattlesnake's Kiss
Small wooden crate (p137)
Pail of water from the well (p148)
Small corked medicine bottle (p150)
Coat (p150)
Cloth to stem the bleeding (p154)
More scraps of cloth to make the bandage (p157)
Carefullt tips contents into a scarp of cloth (p157)
Cigarillo and a pack of matches (p159)
Revolver and reloads a shot (p159)
Old leather duster (p160)
Coat and gun belt (p160)
She reveals a black cloth which she gently ties around his head, covering his eyes (p173)
Shotgun from under the alter (p174)
Revolver (p174)
Wooden crate (p183)

Character/Costume:

Volume I Blood Red Moon
Levi – Well dressed in his winter layers + hat (p25)
Manoah – A strip of black materiel covers his eyes (p26)
Enoch – he's bloodied, bruised and covered in muck. A shotgun is strapped to his back (p72)

Volume II the Clock Strikes Noon
Benjamin Walker – stocky, strong jawed and handsome; he has the look of a man who works outdoors. (p91)

Felix Jackson – appears weak and pale; a 'tin-star' is pinned to his chest (p91)
Manoah – his eyes covered with a black bandage (p92)
Lillian Davenport – She is young and clearly wealthy; her dress, hair and mannerisms appear out of place in this setting (p104)
Lillian – she looks battered and distressed, a spray of blood across her face (p125)

Volume III the Rattlesnake's Kiss
Manoah – a black cloth covers his eyes – he is blind (p137)
Marshall – he is dressed in a smart black suit and the star on his chest indicates he's a law official – US Marshall (p137)
Elena – she appears weary; her skin is dark with dust, her hands cracked and raw from labour (p148)
Jack – He is wounded; a bullet has grazed his right arm (p154)

Lightning

Volume I Blood Red Moon
A soft red glow of moonlight pours in through the crucifix shaped window that stands above the altar. It illuminates the almost derelict building (p25)

Volume II the Clock Strikes Noon
The glow of a late morning sun fills the Chapel of Emmanuel (p91)

Volume III the Rattlesnake's Kiss
Pitch black darkness fills the mines (p162)
The flicker of a candle flame illuminates in the darkness (p166)
The lights starts to fade (p167)
The light fades more (p167)
Darkness has come again (p167)
A flicker of candlelight appears and Elena is there (p171)
Darkness (p185)

Sound Effects

Lightning Source UK Ltd.
Milton Keynes UK
UKOW06f1156190715

255390UK00001B/3/P